CULTURE SMART!

MONGOLIA

Alan Sanders

·K·U·P·E·R·A·R·D·

ISBN 978 1 85733 717 4
This book is also available as an e-book: eISBN 978 1 85733 718 1

British Library Cataloguing in Publication Data
A CIP catalogue entry for this book is available from the
British Library

First published in Great Britain
by Kuperard, an imprint of Bravo Ltd
59 Hutton Grove, London N12 8DS
Tel: +44 (0) 20 8446 2440 Fax: +44 (0) 20 8446 2441
www.culturesmart.co.uk
Inquiries: sales@kuperard.co.uk

Series Editor Geoffrey Chesler
Design Bobby Birchall

Printed in Malaysia

About the Author

ALAN SANDERS is the leading British authority on Mongolia. Formerly the lecturer in Mongolian Studies at London's School of Oriental and African Studies, now, after many years at BBC Monitoring, he is a freelance consultant writing about Mongolia's political and economic scene.

He has written extensively for the weekly *Far Eastern Economic Review*, co-authored the Lonely Planet *Mongolian Phrasebook*, and wrote Routledge's *Colloquial Mongolian*. His *Historical Dictionary of Mongolia* (Scarecrow Press) has gone to three editions, he has updated the Mongolia chapters in the annual *Far East and Australasia* (Europa/Routledge), and revised the online Mongolia for *Encyclopaedia Britannica*.

Alan is a member of the International Association of Mongolian Studies, Ulan Bator, and of the Mongolia Society at Indiana University, and contributes to publications of the Mongolia and Inner Asia Studies Unit, University of Cambridge. He was awarded the Mongolian Order of the Pole Star for promoting British–Mongolian relations.

**The Culture Smart! series is continuing to expand.
For further information and latest titles visit
www.culturesmart.co.uk**

The publishers would like to thank **CultureSmart!**Consulting for its help in researching and developing the concept for this series.

CultureSmart!Consulting creates tailor-made seminars and consultancy programs to meet a wide range of corporate, public-sector, and individual needs. Whether delivering courses on multicultural team building in the USA, preparing Chinese engineers for a posting in Europe, training call-center staff in India, or raising the awareness of police forces to the needs of diverse ethnic communities, it provides essential, practical, and powerful skills worldwide to an increasingly international workforce.

For details, visit www.culturesmartconsulting.com

CultureSmart!Consulting and **CultureSmart!** guides have both contributed to and featured regularly in the weekly travel program "Fast Track" on BBC World TV.

contents

contents

Map of Mongolia

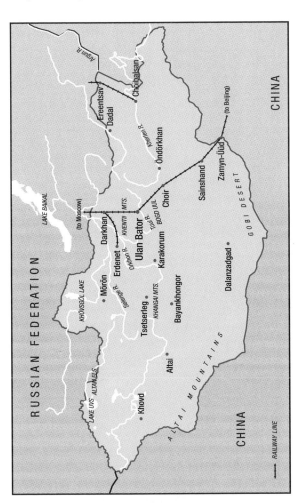

introduction

Mongolia is landlocked between China and Russia in the heart of Asia. For centuries after the disintegration of Genghis Khan's empire it was ruled by one neighbor or the other, but in the 1990s the Mongols abandoned Soviet socialism and turned to democracy. Proud of their heroic past, they are rebuilding their national heritage. During seventy years of Kremlin control, they had gained schools, hospitals, factories, and housing, but lost their freedom, history, religion, and written language. Today they try to preserve a balance with their "eternal neighbors," who inevitably maintain considerable influence, while embracing their "third neighbor"—the United States, Europe, and Japan. In the transition to a market economy Mongolia is a land of pioneers. Its greatest asset is the Mongol people, who are friendly, well educated, and ambitious. The first foreign language, once Russian, is now English. Its business leaders are striving to develop their resource-rich but infrastructure-poor country through international partnerships. The freely elected parliament has formed a series of coalition governments, aiming through consensus and sustainable growth to end poverty and inequality.

Travelers from across the world are drawn to the "land of blue sky" by its picturesque mountains and lakes, flower-carpeted steppes and stony deserts, home to snow leopards, wild horses and camels, and Gobi bears. The broad pasturelands, with herds of grazing livestock and the traditional nomadic lifestyle, contrast remarkably with the busy streets

of the capital. Ulan Bator is a bustling city of over
a million people, modern buildings and shops,
interspersed with Buddhist monasteries and temples
and surrounded by crowded suburbs of traditional felt
tents. *Culture Smart! Mongolia* provides vital insights
and useful tips from an expert's understanding of the
people and the country, rarely in the news but making
steady progress toward democracy and modernity.

Spelling and Names
There is no agreed system for transliterating the
Mongolian Cyrillic alphabet into English spelling.
In this book most of the letters used to reproduce
Mongolian words may be pronounced as in English.
The rest are generally *ch* as in church, *e* = den, *g* = golf,
j = jewel, *kh* = loch, *o* = hot, *ö* = yearn, *ts* = cats, *u* =
awful, *ü* = put, *z* = adze. Vowels with an initial glide,
or y-sound, are *ya* = yard, *ye* = yearn, *yo* = yodel, *yu* =
you, *yü* = yurt. Double vowels are long and stressed:
aa, ee, oo, öö, uu, üü. The letter *v* is between v and w,
except that *govi* is Anglicized as gobi.
  The name of the capital, Ulan Bator, often written
Ulaanbaatar on the basis of the Cyrillic spelling,
is pronounced "Oolahnbarter," with stress on the
second and third syllables. Although the traditional
English spelling is Genghis Khan, the Mongolian
pronunciation Chingis is closer (stress on the first
syllable). The variant Chinggis Khaan is derived from
the classical *uigarjin* script. "Gengis" (hard g) is to be
avoided. Khan is a rank, not a surname.

Key Facts

Country Name	Mongolia	Mongolian People's Republic, 1924–92
Capital	Ulan Bator (Ulaanbaatar)	Pop. 1.3 million
Main Towns	Erdenet, Darkhan	Pop.100,000; 75,000
Population	3.0 million (est. 2014). 66.9% urban, 33.1% rural	Density 1.9 persons per sq. km; average family 3.7 persons
Area	603,909 sq. miles (1,564,116 sq. km)	Mongolia extends for 1,486 miles (2,392 km) west to east, 782 miles (1,259 km) north to south.
Ethnic Makeup	Khalkh Mongols 82.4%; other Mongols 9.9%; Kazakhs 3.9%. Other ethnic groups 3.8% (2010)	Other groups include Turkic and Tungusic tribes; 16,000 foreign residents, mostly Russian or Chinese
Border Countries	Russia to the north, China to the south, east, and west	Landlocked. Main rivers flow northward.
Climate	Long, cold, dry winters and short, warm summers with some rain	Long periods of sunshine; best time to visit June–September
National Bird	Saker falcon, *Idleg shonkhor*	Large falcon used for falconry
Sacred Mountain	Burkhan Khaldun (4,961 ft., 1,512 m)	Genghis Khan's birthplace near Dadal, Dornod aimag
National Flower	Scabiosa comosa, *Ber tsetseg*	A small blue steppe flower
Government	Republic with elected president and monocameral legislature (Great Khural), which appoints the cabinet. Universal suffrage from age 18	

Adult Literacy	Urban 98.3%, rural 96.3% (2010)	Students graduating 37,243 (2013)
Languages	Khalkh Mongol is the state language. Kazakh predominates in northwestern Mongolia.	English has overtaken Russian as the first foreign language; neither is widely understood in the countryside.
Religion	Lamaism, Gelugpa Buddhism headed by the Dalai Lama (36.6%); Islam (2.1%); Shamanism (2%); Christianity (1.5%)	Mongolia was ruled 1924–90 by a communist party that banned all religious activity and promoted atheism.
Age Structure	Under 14, 20%; 15–64, 76%; 65 and over, 4%	Life expectancy at birth: males 65.4 years, females 75 years
GDP Per Capita	US $3,964 (2013)	Inflation 11% (2014)
Currency	Tugrik (*tögrög*) (MNT)	US $1=MNT 1,975 (April 2015)
Electricity	220 volts, 50 Hz	Two-prong plug
Video/TV	PAL	Digitalization by 2016
Internet Domain	.mn or .gov.mn	Companies use .com, .org, and .net
Telephone	Country code 976; Ulan Bator 11, 21, or 51 for landlines, not for eight-digit cell phone numbers	To call out, 00 followed by international country code
Time Zones	Ulan Bator, central and eastern provinces, GMT + 8 hrs	Three westernmost provinces, GMT + 7 hrs

chapter one

LAND &
PEOPLE

GEOGRAPHY

An independent landlocked country in the heart
of Asia between N41° and 52° and E88° and 120°,
Mongolia borders Russia (RF) for 2,202 miles
(3,543 km) to the north and China (PRC) for 2,926 miles
(4,709 km) to the east, south, and west. Mongolia's area
of 603,909 square miles (1,564,116 sq. km) makes it
the eighteenth-largest country in the world, but with a
population of three million the average density is fewer
than five persons per square mile (or 2 per sq. km). The
capital, Ulan Bator (Ulaanbaatar), 4,400 feet (1,350 m)
above sea level, has a population of 1.3 million.

The western and northern borders and central plateau
are mountainous, the south and east flat, mostly steppe

and *govi* (gobi), or gravel semi-desert. The highest
peak, Khüiten ("cold"), rises to 14,355 feet (4,374 m) at
the western junction of Mongolia's borders with China
and Russia in the Tavan Bogd ("holy five") range of
the Mongol Altai Mountains. The lowest point is Lake
Khökhnuur (1,745 feet, or 532 m. above sea level) in the
eastern plains, but the biggest lakes are in the west and
north: Lake Uvs (1,446 sq. miles, or 3,376 sq. km), and
Lake Khövsgöl (1,057 sq. miles, or 2,738 sq. km). The
longest river, the Kherlen, 754 miles (1,213 km), rises
in the northern Khentii Mountains, loops east and, via
Chinese Inner Mongolia, joins the Argun tributary of
the Amur (Heilongjiang, Black Dragon River) forming
the Russian–Chinese border. The Orkhon, 698 miles
(1,124 km), rises in the Khangai Mountains and flows
north, near the Russian border joining the Selenge,
which enters Lake Baikal.

Forest, mostly Siberian larch, covers about 8 percent
of Mongolia, mainly on the northern mountain slopes.
Some 36 percent is desert and *govi*, but dunes form only
a small proportion. The Gobi mesas are the source of
dinosaur fossils and eggs. Altan Els ("golden sands"),

east of Lake Uvs, is the world's northernmost desert. The steppe, which accounts for 55 percent of the country, is where most nomads live, in *ger*, or circular, felt-covered, lattice-walled tents, grazing their herds of sheep, goats, cattle, horses, and camels (52 million head at the end of 2014).

Mongolia's continental climate has long, cold winters and short, hot summers. Ulan Bator's average January temperature is -40°F (-40°C) and its July average 63°F (17°C). Spring is windy and dusty; summer downpours can flood rivers. In winter frozen snow may cover pastures, so livestock cannot graze and would starve if not moved or fed emergency fodder.

THE PEOPLE

Mongols

Genghis Khan united Turkic and Tungusic "people of the felt tents" as the Mongol nation in 1206. Because of his belief in "eternal blue heaven" (see Tengerism, page 51), Genghis called his people "Blue Mongols." They are born with a blue spot (*khökh tolbo*) on the buttocks, a common feature of Japanese and Koreans. After the Mongol Empire's collapse the heartland was incorporated in the Qing Empire of China's Manchu conquerors, the southern Mongols' territory as Inner Mongolia, and the northern Mongols' lands as Outer Mongolia. Russia expanded into Siberia, bringing the Buryats at Lake Baikal under the Tsar's rule. The Oirats, or western Mongols, were destroyed by the Qing as a political power, but remain a distinctive cultural group. The Kalmyks fled Qing China and migrated to Russia, occupying the Caspian steppes. Outer Mongolia came under Soviet control in 1921,

while Inner Mongolia remained part of China. The world population of Mongols is estimated at nine million, and more live outside Mongolia than in it. The Mongol population of China's Inner Mongolia Autonomous Region alone is more numerous, although a minority among the Han Chinese. Most Mongols living in Mongolia today are Khalkh, constituting 82.4 percent of the population (2010). The largest Mongol minorities are Dörvöd (2.8 percent) in the northwest, and Buryat (1.7 percent) along the Russian border.

Kazakhs

Living as nomads in the Altai Mountain borderlands of China in the nineteenth century, Kazakh tribes moved into western Mongolia, where they constitute the majority in Bayan-Ölgii province and a significant minority in neighboring Khovd and Uvs provinces. They account for 3.9 percent of Mongolia's population (2010). Some

Kazakhs claim descent from Genghis Khan's eldest son, Jochi. The word Kazakh (*qazaq*), meaning "marauder," comes from the fourteenth century and is also the source of the Russian word Cossack. In the twentieth century Mongolia's Kazakhs worked in the coalmines of Nalaikh and Darkhan. Many of Bayan-Ölgii's Kazakhs are herders; some are hunters with eagles.

After the birth of democracy in Mongolia in 1990, thousands of Kazakhs emigrated to Kazakhstan, but many later returned. Mongolia's Kazakhs speak a dialect of the same Altaic language as the Kazakhs of Kazakhstan, but their speech and customs were hardly understood there, and they found assimilation difficult.

The Turkic minorities of Mongolia include the Khoton, perhaps of Uighur origin, living in Uvs province, and the Tannu Uriankhai or Dukhan reindeer herders of the Lake Khövsgöl area, related to the Tuvans of the neighboring RF Republic of Tuva.

Language

The official language of the country is Mongol, and its Khalkh dialect is spoken by 80 percent of the population. Other dialects are spoken in neighboring countries. Mongol is a Ural-Altaic language and most closely resembles the Turkic languages of some Central Asian republics and Turkey. Tibetan, Chinese, and Russian terms have been absorbed over the centuries.

Mongol is unusual in having two scripts. The Mongolian Cyrillic alphabet was adopted for everyday use after the Second World War. The earlier "Uighur" syllabary, written in vertical columns, was introduced under Genghis Khan. It was banned during the Soviet period, and revived after the birth of democracy in 1990. While Mongolia was "building socialism" after the Second World War the second language of Mongols was Russian, which was taught in all schools. Today the foreign language of choice is English.

Because Kazakh is not an official language in Mongolia, Mongolia's Kazakhs have to use Mongol in contacts with the authorities. For a brief description of languages and scripts, see page 152.

A BRIEF HISTORY
The Founding State

The 2,220th anniversary of Modun Shanyui's proclamation of the Hun state in 209 BCE was decreed by Mongolian President Elbegdorj in 2011 as the anniversary of the "founding state" of the Mongols, and the Huns (Khünnü, Xiongnu) are considered the Mongols' ancestors. Our knowledge about them comes mostly from the archaeology of northern Mongolia. The Hun state disintegrated in the fourth century CE, and in the sixth to seventh centuries Turkic people ruled what is now Mongolia, commemorating their kings and generals in runic inscriptions. They were succeeded by the Uighurs (744–840), who built their capital in the Orkhon Valley and became allies of Tang China. The Uighurs were displaced by the nomadic Yenisei Kirghiz, who in turn were dispersed in 920 by the Qidan, a sinicized Mongol tribe, which established the Liao dynasty (947–1125). This was ended by the Tungusic Jurchen people, related to the Manchu, whose Jin ("golden") dynasty ruled northern China (1115–1234). The Jin archives recorded an early Mongol state called Mengfuguo, perhaps the Khamag Mongol Uls (state of all the Mongols) of Qabul Khan, which collapsed in 1160.

THE CHARACTER OF GENGHIS KHAN

History and legend combine in the *Secret History of the Mongols,* the oldest known Mongolian account of the life of Genghis Khan, probably completed in the Year of the Rat (1228). A text in Mongol, written in Chinese characters, was discovered by a Russian Orthodox missionary in Beijing in 1872. No original text of the *Secret History* in Mongol script has been found, although extracts exist in later manuscripts. The *Secret History* gives the ancestors of Genghis Khan as Börte Chino and Qo'ai Maral, a wolf and a doe (or people with these names), and recounts episodes from the lives of several generations. Genghis Khan was born, it says, "with his destiny ordained by eternal heaven," the son of the Mongol chieftain Yesügei, who named him Temüüjin ("blacksmith") after a defeated Tatar enemy. Historians have determined the year as 1162, but sources differ as to the date, which was determined according to the lunar calendar. It is thought that he was born on the first day of the first winter month (November), when his birthday is now celebrated.

Temüüjin was eight years old when his father was poisoned by Tatars, and he, his mother, and his younger brothers were abandoned by their family. The *Secret History* tells how, having learned as a boy the skills of physical survival and building alliances, as a young man he taught himself military tactics and political diplomacy. Temüüjin was proclaimed *khan* of all the Mongols in 1189, and once he had united the "people of the felt tents" in 1206 he adopted the title of Genghis Khan, meaning almighty, or "world ruler".

Historians of the countries conquered by the armies of Genghis Khan tended to emphasize the destructive power and military skill of the Mongols, the sacking of ancient cities and the terrible loss of life. Genghis Khan's definition of "supreme joy," according to the Persian contemporary historian Rashid al-Din, was "to cut my enemies to pieces, drive them before me, seize their possessions, witness the tears of their dear ones, and embrace their wives and daughters."

In contrast, the *Secret History* portrays him as a careful planner, astute politician, and great leader and lawmaker. His rules demanded loyalty, but he did not always follow them. Now that Genghis Khan can be admired again, after the years of socialist rule in Mongolia under Soviet guidance, in the country's biggest statue of him, on the capital's main square now named after him, he is portrayed not in armor on horseback, but enthroned.

Genghis Khan may even have had a sense of humor. He is said to have remarked: "If a man gets drunk more than twice a month, he is guilty of a punishable offense. If he is drunk only twice a month, that is better; if only once a month, that is praiseworthy. What could be better than he should not drink at all? But where shall we find a man who never drinks?"

The Mongol Empire (1207–1368)

Genghis Khan's conquests began in 1207 with invasion of the Xi Xia (Tangut) state in northern China. Neighboring Tibet agreed to pay tribute and was not invaded. Genghis captured the Jin capital Kaiping (1215), invaded Khorazm (1219), seized Bukhara and Samarkand (1220), invaded Georgia and Crimea (1221), and defeated the Russian knights on the River Kalka near Donetsk (1223). After returning to Mongolia, he reinvaded Xi Xia, where he died in 1227. His body was taken to Mongolia for secret burial.

Genghis Khan held assemblies (*quriltai*) to consult his senior commanders, and after his death they continued as councils of nobles, nominating the new ruler. Genghis was succeeded as the second Great Khan (1228) by his third son Ögödei, who built Karakorum. After Genghis's death Tibet ceased paying tribute, and was invaded in 1240 by Ögödei Khan's son Köten (Godan). He invited the Tibetan Sakya Pandita, Abbot of Sakya "red hat" monastery, to become religious adviser to the Mongols, establishing the "patron–priest" relationship. He set out in 1244 for Köten's camp at Kokonor (Qinghai), bordering on Tibet, but they met only in 1247, in Lanzhou. The Sakya Pandita died in 1251 and his remains are preserved in the White Pagoda monastery near Lake Qinghai. The PRC claims this as proof that Tibet was under China's jurisdiction.

During Ögödei's reign, Genghis's grandson Batu Khan destroyed Vladimir and other Russian cities, and in December 1240 besieged Kiev, breached the walls, and slaughtered the inhabitants. Batu ruled a vast territory from the Irtysh to the Volga Rivers and the Caucasus. His *ulus* (appanage) was called the Golden Horde after the Khan's golden-yellow tent-palace (*ord*). In 1243 he established his capital at Sarai-Batu on the Akhtuba River, near modern Astrakhan.

After Ögödei's death in 1241 there was a five-year regency by his widow. His eldest son, Güyüg, was proclaimed the third Great Khan in 1246. Batu refused to recognize him, and Güyüg, on his way from Mongolia to confront Batu, died in Samarkand. He was succeeded in 1251 by his cousin Möngke as the fourth Great Khan. Möngke's brother Khülegü conquered Iran, besieged the castles of the assassins, captured Baghdad in 1258, and destroyed the Abbasid caliphate. Another brother, Kublai, replaced Köten at Kokonor and invited the Sakya Pandita's nephew, Phagspa Lama, to join him in a new "patron–priest" relationship. In 1254 the Phagspa Lama was given supreme authority over Tibet.

Möngke died in China fighting troops of the Song dynasty (960–1279), which was overthrown by Kublai Khan. Kublai succeeded him as the fifth Great Khan in 1264, after defeating another brother, Arigbökh, based in Karakorum. Kublai's base at Kaiping was renamed Shangdu (upper capital, Coleridge's Xanadu), the summer capital near Dolonnor (Duolun). In 1267 Kublai moved to Zhongdu (middle capital) and renamed it Dadu (great capital), now Beijing. Marco Polo called it Cambaluc or the "Khan's City." In 1276 Mongol troops in south China captured the emperor of the so-called Southern Song dynasty (1127–1276), overthrowing it, and Mongol troops invaded Burma in 1277. Kublai's first attempt to invade Japan in 1274 failed, and the fleet assembled in Korea for another invasion in 1281 was dispersed by a typhoon. Kublai proclaimed himself Emperor Shi Zu of the Yuan dynasty, the first foreign dynasty to rule China, in 1280, and died in 1294.

The last Yuan Emperor, Togoon Tömör Khan, was driven from Beijing in 1368 by the Ming Emperor Taizu. Togoon Tömör died in Inner Mongolia and his son was enthroned at Karakorum, which Ming troops destroyed in 1380. Timur the Lame (Tamerlane) set out to restore the Mongol Empire in Samarkand in 1360, conquered Iran, Mesopotamia, and Khorazm, invaded India in 1398, seized Ankara from the Ottomans in 1402, and died in 1406 campaigning against the Ming. Their struggle to subdue the Mongols continued under Emperor Yongle (1403–24). The Russian Grand Duke Dmitri "Donskoi" defeated the Golden Horde at Kulikovo Pole in 1380. The Russian princes stopped paying tribute, and in 1480 Ivan III drove the Golden Horde out of Russia.

The Manchu Empire (1636–1911)

Altan Khan of the Tumet Mongols made peace with the Ming and in 1554 founded, in Inner Mongolia, his capital Khökhkhot, or "blue town," after the glazed tiles set in the walls. In 1559 he set off on a campaign against the Kokonor Mongols. In Tibet the Gelugpa or "yellow hat" order had become established, and Altan Khan invited the Abbot of Sera monastery to meet him at Kokonor in 1578. Altan Khan converted to the "yellow" faith and named the abbot "Dalai Lama." They agreed they must be incarnations of Kublai Khan and the Phagspa Lama. The abbot became the third Dalai Lama, as there had been two previous incarnations.

In Russia's conquest of Asia the Cossacks made their way eastward along Siberian rivers, demanding tribute in furs, founding Tobolsk (1587), Krasnoyarsk (1627), and Irkutsk (1661), and reaching Lake Baikal. Meanwhile, in northern China, the Manchu Great Khan Nurhachi established his capital at Mukden (Shenyang) in 1625, and his successor Abahai named his dynasty the Qing in 1636. The last Mongol Great Khan, Ligden Khan of the Chakhar, died in 1634 before he could form an alliance with the Ming against the Manchu. The Manchu challenged Russian penetration of eastern Siberia north of the Amur (Heilongjiang), and in 1685 destroyed Fort Albazin. Their eastern border was agreed upon in 1689 at Nerchinsk, in the first treaty ever signed by China's rulers. The Manchu took control of southern (Inner) Mongolia in 1636.

The monk, scholar, and artist Zanabazar, son of the Khalkh Mongol Tüsheet Khan, a descendant of Genghis Khan, was recognized in 1639 at the age of five as an incarnation of the Tibetan scholar Javzandamba. He adopted the title Öndör Gegeen (High Enlightened One), and visited Tibet to meet the Dalai Lama and Panchen Lama. When, with the unifying presence of the Great Khan gone, the Oirats attacked the Khalkh in 1687, the Öndör Gegeen recommended seeking Manchu protection. In 1691 at Dolonnor the Qing Emperor Kangxi accepted the allegiance of the Khalkh whose territory became Outer Mongolia. The Mongols considered their relationship with the Qing an alliance, but once the Manchu had put a stop to Oirat attacks they absorbed Mongolia into their military–administrative structure, replacing Mongol law with Manchu law and stationing Manchu governors in Uliastai and Khovd. Mongol trade with Russia was banned.

Russia's border treaty with the Qing, signed in 1727 at Kyakhta, confirmed Qing control over Mongolia and Uriankhai (Tuva).

Zanabazar's nomadic palace (*örgöö*) was replaced in 1706 by a nomadic great monastery (*ikh khüree*), which in 1778 settled in the Tuul Valley; both names were used to mean the "capital." The first permanent temple buildings were erected in 1837 where Ulan Bator now stands. The Mongol people were oppressed and impoverished by greedy princes and traders, and subjected to cruel punishments, imprisoned in wooden chests or locked into *cangues* (heavy wooden collars). Weakened by the Taiping (1851) and Boxer (1900) rebellions, foreign intervention, mutinies, and uprisings, Qing rule collapsed.

Autonomous Mongolia (1911–19)

In December 1911 the eighth Öndör Gegeen was proclaimed Bogd Khan (Holy King) of Mongolia and declared Mongolia's independence, but foreign states

failed to respond. Ikh Khüree was renamed Niislel Khüree ("capital monastery"). General Yuan Shih-k'ai, proclaimed President of China, retained control over Inner Mongolia. Outer Mongolia signed a treaty with Russia in 1912 and Prime Minister Namnansüren visited Russia in 1913–14. Mongolia and Tibet concluded a treaty of mutual recognition. Outer Mongolia had been granted autonomy in internal affairs by a Russian–Chinese treaty in 1913, but was obliged to accept Chinese suzerainty under the 1915 tripartite Treaty of Kyakhta. The Soviet Russian government recognized the Bogd Khan in 1919, but Chinese troops invaded and reimposed rule from Beijing.

In April 1920 Mongol revolutionaries joined forces to found the Mongolian People's Party (MPP) in the Russian town of Troitskosavsk (Kyakhta). Contact was established with Russian Bolsheviks, but in October 1920 White Russian Cossack cavalry, commanded by the Baltic German Baron Roman von Ungern-Sternberg, entered eastern Mongolia from Chita, drove the Chinese out of Niislel Khüree, and restored the Bogd Khan.

The Mongolian Revolution

The MPP's first congress, held in March 1921 in Kyakhta, set up a provisional government and proclaimed unity, freedom, self-government, and friendship with the revolutionary parties of Russia and China. Mongolian cavalry, supported by Soviet troops, took Niislel Khüree (July 11). Ungern was captured and in Novonikolayevsk (Novosibirsk) executed by a Bolshevik tribunal for "armed counter-revolution." Revolutionary leaders Bodoo and Sükhbaatar became prime minister and commander-in-chief. The political commissar of the army, Choibalsan, was made leader of the Revolutionary Youth League. The Bogd Khan was enthroned, but with limited powers. Lenin received a Mongolian delegation in Moscow and the first Mongolian–Soviet Treaty was signed in November 1921, the governments recognizing each other as the only legal authority in their country. Lenin urged the Mongols to follow the "path of non-capitalist development."

Bodoo was shot for "counter-revolutionary activity" in August 1922, and Sükhbaatar died in February 1923. The MPP's second congress in July 1923 called for the strengthening of friendship with Soviet Russia. When the Bogd Khan died in May the search for his reincarnation was banned. The MPP's third congress in August 1924 followed Lenin's path of "bypassing capitalism," and the word "revolutionary" was added to the party's name. During the congress the deputy prime minister, Danzan, was executed for allegedly "representing bourgeois interests" and "harming friendship" with the Soviets, although as a top revolutionary party leader he had signed the Mongolian–Soviet friendship treaty with Lenin in November 1921, and served as Minister of Finance 1921–23, and Commander-in-Chief 1923–24. After military training in Russia, Choibalsan became commander-in-chief. In November a national assembly, the Great Khural, adopted the first constitution, naming the country the Mongolian People's Republic (MPR). Niislel Khüree was renamed Ulan Bator, town of the "Red Hero(es)." Mongolia joined Bolshevik Russia in signing a friendship treaty with the People's Republic of Tuva in 1926.

The Road to Stalinism
The fifth congress of the Mongolian People's Republican Party (MPRP) in 1926 nationalized private property and accused "Rightists" of encouraging capitalism, undermining relations with the USSR, and opposing the Comintern. The MPRP's seventh congress in 1928 defeated "Right opportunists," but in 1929 new leaders expropriated monastery property and forced herdsmen into communes. There were "counter-revolutionary uprisings" at monasteries, and herdsmen slaughtered their livestock. In a May 1932 intervention, the Comintern and

Soviet Communist Party instructed the MPRP to expel "Left deviationists," and a moderate "New Turn" was proclaimed.

The following period was marked by the rise of Choibalsan, first deputy chairman of the Council of Ministers, 1935–39, and Minister of Internal Affairs, 1936–40. In the purges of 1937–39 some 30,000 people were arrested on trumped-up charges of "counter-revolution," or "espionage" for Japan, and most of them shot. The victims were buried in unmarked mass graves. Buddhist clergy were subjected to "show trials" in the Green Dome Theater on Ulan Bator's main square. Prime Ministers Genden (1932–36) and Amar (1936–39), were arrested by the NKVD (the Soviet secret police), and tried and shot in Moscow.

International Recognition
Japan had occupied parts of China and created the puppet state of Manchukuo in northwest China and Inner Mongolia in 1932. Choibalsan was appointed Minister of War in 1937. In July 1939 Japanese troops invaded eastern Mongolia, were beaten back, but brought up reinforcements. In the Battle of Khalkhyn Gol

(Nomonhan) in August, after heavy fighting involving armor and aircraft, the Japanese–Manchukuo forces were defeated by Mongolian–Soviet units under General Zhukov, and an armistice was agreed.

Mongolia did not declare war against Nazi Germany, but from 1943 contributed 300 kg of gold, US $100,000, horses, livestock, meat, and uniforms to the Soviet war effort, and paid for 32 T-34 tanks and 12 La-5 fighter planes. In 1944 the USSR turned the "people's republic" of Tuva into an administrative district of Russia.

At the Yalta conference in 1945 President Roosevelt, Prime Minister Churchill, and Marshal Stalin—not yet a Generalissimo (the title was awarded for winning the war)—agreed that, in exchange for the US and UK accepting the status quo in Mongolia, the USSR would enter the war against Japan. In August 1945 Mongolian troops joined the Red Army's invasion of northeast China. The Republic of China (RoC) accepted the Yalta agreement subject to a plebiscite in Mongolia. It was held in October 1945, the Mongols voting 100 percent for independence, and the RoC recognized the MPR in January 1946.

On the proclamation of the People's Republic of China (PRC) in 1949 Stalin transferred Soviet recognition to the PRC, and Mongolia followed suit. In October 1961, after several unsuccessful applications, the MPR joined the United Nations. The UK, in 1963, was the first West European country to establish diplomatic relations with Mongolia.

Stalin's death in March 1953 was followed by First Secretary Khrushchev's anti-Stalin speech at the CPSU congress in 1956. Prime Minister Malenkov was made manager of a power station, and his ally Foreign Minister Molotov was appointed ambassador to Mongolia.

The growing dispute between the USSR and the PRC over leadership of the communist movement led to confrontation. From the late 1950s Chairman Mao directly challenged the post-Stalin interpretation of Marxism–Leninism and split the communist movement. Polycentrism became the dominant feature of interparty relations, the notion that each party could best judge the appropriate road to communism, rather than slavishly applying the Soviet model.

The USSR feared Chinese invasion, and Soviet Party leader Brezhnev visited Ulan Bator in 1966 to sign a new Mongolian–Soviet Treaty with a secret annex, allowing the USSR to station troops in Mongolia in response to the Chinese "threat." In 1969 fighting broke out across the Soviet–Chinese border on the Ussuri River. In 1971 Mao's "heir apparent," Lin Piao, was killed when his military transport jet crashed in Mongolia. Border tension continued through the 1970s, and many of Mongolia's Chinese residents were expelled. The Chinese authorities revised the internal boundaries of Inner Mongolia and the Mongol population was withdrawn from border areas.

Brezhnev launched a drive for détente with the West in the early 1970s. Chairman Mao died in September 1976. In 1979 China stopped calling the Soviets "revisionists," and in 1984 began to downplay the Soviet danger. In 1986 the new Soviet leader Gorbachev, in a speech in Vladivostok on Asia–Pacific security, disclosed that the withdrawal of Soviet troops from Mongolia was under discussion. The PRC leaders recognized Mongolia's independence and territorial integrity, and normalized relations. The US recognized the PRC in 1978, and established diplomatic relations with Mongolia in January 1987.

Russification

The MPRP General Secretary Tsedenbal, who had succeeded Prime Minister Choibalsan in 1952, ordered the official celebration in 1962 of the 800th anniversary of Genghis Khan's birth, including building a monument at his birthplace. When the Soviet *Pravda* criticized the "Mongol–Tatar Empire which placed Russia under its yoke," the Mongolian Politburo abandoned the celebration and fired the member in charge. (The monument still stands.)

Tsedenbal became head of state in 1974. His wife was Russian, and they got along well with Brezhnev, whose pretensions Tsedenbal copied. He had received his first Order of Lenin from Stalin in 1944, and for his sixtieth birthday in 1976 Brezhnev gave him another. Tsedenbal promoted himself Army General, and in 1979 awarded himself the rank of Marshal, once used by Choibalsan. In March 1981 Mongolia's cosmonaut Gürragchaa spent eight days in space, aboard the Soviet Salyut-6 space station. Tsedenbal made him a Hero of the MPR and shared his glory. In December 1981 Tsedenbal launched a campaign to "root out the weeds" in the MPRP, and dismissed the President of the Academy of Sciences.

Tsedenbal was in Moscow in August 1984 when the Mongolian Politburo announced his removal from the posts of Party General Secretary and head of state "on account of his health, and with his agreement." He was held responsible for Mongolia's "stagnation," stripped of his Party membership and medals, and exiled in Moscow, where he died in 1991. He was buried in Ulan Bator. When President Bagabandi and the MPRP tried to restore his reputation, ex-President Ochirbat commented: "His rehabilitation would once again blacken the names of those [victims] who have justly been rehabilitated."

The Birth of Democracy
Under the 1960 Constitution the MPRP was the "guiding and directing force of society," but in 1989 Mongolian students, encouraged by social movements stirring in Eastern Europe, began forming "unofficial" political groups. Tsedenbal's successor, Batmönkh, tried to follow Gorbachev's policy of *perestroika*, but senior MPRP members expressed concern about "extreme nationalism." There was renewed interest in Genghis Khan and Mongolian history, and popular demands to reevaluate Mongol–Soviet relations. After the fall of the Berlin wall Mongolian students called on the MPRP leaders to resign. Having tried to calm demonstrators in Ulan Bator by ordering the removal of Stalin's statue from outside the State Library, the Politburo finally resigned in March 1990. The Great Khural deleted the "guiding force" from the constitution, political parties were legalized, and the Ministry of Public Security abolished. Further constitutional amendments created, as an interim solution, an enlarged Great Khural of 430 elected delegates and a standing legislature, the Little Khural of fifty members elected by proportional representation, where the Democrats and allies took nineteen seats.

GOVERNMENT AND POLITICS
The New Constitution
Mongolia's fourth constitution, adopted in January 1992, gave priority to human rights and created a new assembly, the seventy-six-seat Great Khural, elected in June for a four-year term. The MPRP with 57 percent of the ballot won seventy-one seats, and the anti-MPRP coalition with 40 percent won five. In 1993, the Democratic candidate Ochirbat won the first direct presidential election. An

alliance of national and social democrats won the 1996 Great Khural election, but the MPRP took seventy-two seats in the 2000 election.

The 2004 Great Khural election result was almost a dead heat and the MPRP and Motherland–Democracy alliance formed a coalition headed by Prime Minister Elbegdorj. After the MPRP won the 2008 Great Khural election a mob burned down its headquarters; a state of emergency and curfew were declared in Ulan Bator. In September the MPRP formed a "joint" government with the Democratic Party (DP).

The President

Elected directly for a four-year term, the president may be reelected once. Presidential candidates, Mongolian citizens at least forty-five years old, are nominated by political parties, but on election suspend membership and swear to defend the rights of all citizens. The president is commander-in-chief of the armed forces and chairs the National Security Council, whose other members are the speaker of the Great Khural and the prime minister. Presidents may initiate legislation, and President Elbegdorj, elected in June 2009, announced in early 2010 the suspension of capital punishment, pending abolition. He was reelected in 2013, and the inauguration was held in public, before Genghis Khan's statue.

Parliament

Initially the seats in the Great Khural were filled by simple majority election in twenty-six multiple-seat constituencies, later in seventy-six single-seat constituencies. In 2012 partial proportional representation was introduced, with twenty-eight seats filled from party lists. Electronic machines were brought

in for voting. Five of Mongolia's twenty-two political parties are represented in parliament. The majority party (currently the DP) or coalition in the Great Khural forms the government.

The Mongolian People's Party (MPP), Mongolia's oldest political party, founded in 1920, added the word "revolutionary" to its name in 1925, but in November 2010 the MPRP opted to revert to MPP. Objecting members resigned to form a new MPRP. From 2012 the DP was in coalition with the Civil Courage–Green Party and Justice, itself a coalition of the new MPRP and the National Democratic Party. In November 2014 the DP expanded the coalition to include the MPP, leaving three Independents as the "opposition." All governments formed since 2004 have been coalitions.

Administration

Mongolia is divided into the capital territory and twenty-one provinces (*aimag*) subdivided into some three hundred rural districts (*sum*). Ulan Bator comprises nine urban districts (*düüreg*), three being separate townships, and the "governor of the capital territory" is also mayor of Ulan Bator. Provincial governors are elected by the majority in the provincial assemblies, and appointed by the prime minister.

THE ECONOMY
Introduction
A century ago Mongolian people who were not lamas or nobles were *khamjlaga* (serfs) or *albat* ("taxables"), serving in the army or working in the horse relay stations that supplied mounts for official messengers. Those who owned no livestock looked after the livestock of others, traveled with caravans, or did manual labor. There were a few foreign-owned gold mines. The first industrial enterprises were built after 1921 by the USSR. The labor force and its output were small, and most transport was horse-drawn. In the 1930s and '40s the USSR built the first schools and hospitals. Ulan Bator developed as the administrative center, with state-owned enterprises producing building materials, textiles, chinaware, and so on. Soviet geologists carried out extensive studies of Mongolia's mineral resources. Nalaikh coalmine was modernized, with a narrow-gauge railway to Ulan Bator. The founding of the Comecon (CMEA) in 1949 encouraged financial and economic cooperation and mutual aid with East European partners.

Three important economic projects matured in Mongolia in the 1950s and '60s: the Ulan Bator Railway (UBR); Mongolia's first new industrial town, Darkhan; and a copper mine at Erdenet. The Russian broad-gauge, single-track branch line from the Trans-Siberian Railway, built by Soviet political prisoners, reached Ulan Bator in 1949; the extension to the southern border and Beijing was completed by China in 1955. At Zamyn-Üüd there is a freight trans-shipment center where the wheels on passenger coaches are switched to China's standard gauge. The UBR, now a Mongolian–Russian joint stock company, carries some twenty million metric tons of freight a year, mostly coal and minerals. Darkhan was founded in 1961 on the railway north of Ulan Bator and has a branch line from Sharyn Gol coalmine. Darkhan's factories produce building materials, iron castings, woolen textiles, carpets, flour, and other foodstuffs. There is a cement works at nearby Salkhit, the junction for Erdenet. The joint Soviet–Mongolian copper and molybdenum mine at Erdenet produced twenty-nine million metric tons of copper ore in 2014.

Bypassing Socialism
After the birth of democracy in 1990, Mongolia decided not to "bypass capitalism" but to develop a market economy. First housing and small businesses were privatized. Herding cooperatives and state farms were broken up and the livestock passed into private hands. By 2013 there were 794,100 households countrywide, including 145,300 herder households, with most families owning around two to three hundred head. Laws on land ownership were adopted in 2002.

From early 1991 the USSR made Mongolia settle its trade payments in US dollars. When the USSR disintegrated in August 1991 most economic cooperation ceased and Mongolia became dependent on aid from the US and Japan, the World Bank, and the International Monetary Fund. In December 2003 Russia announced Mongolia's "settlement" for US $250m of the "big debt" owed for Soviet aid 1945–90, of which 98 percent had been written off. An outstanding "final payment" was settled in 2009.

From Aid to Investment

The millennium saw the transition from foreign aid to foreign investment, attracted to Mongolia by its mineral wealth. Rio Tinto's Oyuu Tolgoi opencast copper and gold mine, near the border with China, has doubled Mongolia's copper concentrate production. However, squabbles over the state's eventual 34 percent ownership of Oyuu Tolgoi,

its development costs, and taxation, have delayed the opening up of even richer underground deposits. Commercial uncertainty and falling commodity prices led to a sharp decline in Mongolia's FDI (foreign direct investment) in 2012–14.

Development of the state-owned Tavan Tolgoi coalfield helps to satisfy China's enormous appetite to feed its power stations and industry. After a fall in the international price of coal, Tavan Tolgoi was unable (2015) to reach agreement with the Chinese company Chalco, its main client, on loan repayment. Meanwhile, the development focus has been moving back to agriculture and tourism, which is a growth industry. Foreign tourist numbers are planned to reach one million a year by 2020.

THE ENVIRONMENT

Most damage to the environment is done by wind erosion of the soil and the encroachment of desert, which can be limited by planting shelterbelts. Coal and oil exports to China have depended on convoys of twelve-wheeler trucks driven across the steppe to border delivery points, churning up the surface, pending construction of hard roads. The "Green Wall" national program is planting trees in eighty-nine districts of fourteen provinces. Mining companies usually undertake restorative earthworks and plant trees on the land they have disturbed. Small artisanal mining operations can be harmful to Mongolia's environment. Freelance miners, called "ninjas," scavenging uncontrolled in commercially worked-out gold fields, destroy animal and plant life by digging holes and diverting and polluting rivers.

Pollution

Ulan Bator's housing shortage has resulted in the rapid spread of unlicensed housing and unsatisfied demand for drinking water, power, and sewerage, as well as traffic jams and exhaust fumes. Smog from urban power stations is compounded by tens of thousands of *ger* dwellers burning cheap coal in iron stoves for heating and cooking. Refuse collection tends to be haphazard, and rubbish and building waste simply dumped. Along the rutted tracks that pass for roads in much of the countryside, wheels, worn tires, and other vehicle parts lie where they were abandoned. In forest areas trees are cut down illegally for firewood.

Protection and Hunting

Bogd Khan Mountain, south of Ulan Bator, is said to have been under official protection since 1778. The Great Gobi Strictly Protected Area was registered in 1975, followed by national conservation parks, like Lake Khövsgöl, and nature reserves, in 1995. The Ministry of Environment publishes the *Red Book of Mongolia* on protection of endangered species. Commercial hunters are allowed to take fox, sable, squirrel, and other fur-bearing animals, and sell falcons to the Arab world. Small annual quotas of approved species, such as ibex, wild sheep, deer, boar, and wolf are licensed for foreign hunters.

chapter two

VALUES &
ATTITUDES

The Mongol people's hopes and wishes for the future are closely tied to traditional values such as loyalty to family and clan and respect for elders and religion, although these values were undermined during the years of "building socialism" under Soviet guidance (1921–90). Mongol society, overwhelmingly Buddhist, was forced by the new communist rulers to abandon its old faith and accept new values, ranging from the propaganda of atheism and one-party rule to alliance with Russia and the Marxist doctrine of dictatorship of the proletariat, although at that time Mongolia had no proletariat. The Russians also taught the Mongols to drink vodka.

The population may be divided into urban (educated, housed, and wage-earning) and rural (uneducated, nomadic, and measuring wealth in livestock). The people hope to gain from the world's interest in Mongolia's mineral wealth, but the state has little money of its own to invest, and there is some reluctance to allow foreigners to "steal" the country's resources. This attitude reflects the anti-Western views of the socialist period, but in the times of the Mongol conquests army commanders shared the spoils of war with their officers and men, on the march accompanied by their families, with their homes and livestock. Sharing wealth among themselves is traditional.

History and twentieth-century politics have left the Mongols confused and divided. There is no more empire, but they have won back Genghis Khan as their national hero. The cult of the political leader continues, because of the older generation's nostalgia for the communist past. Then, as one historian remarked, "Only the future was certain, the past was changing all the time." Ulan Bator's Stalin and Lenin monuments have gone, but Marshal Choibalsan, Mongolia's Stalin, responsible for the death of perhaps 30,000 people in the purges of the 1930s, still stands outside the National University. The statue of another dictator, Mongolia's Brezhnev, "Marshal" Tsedenbal, sitting in Drama Theater Square, is a reminder of their divided past: those who supported him in all things Russian and want to "restore his honor," and those who have been rehabilitated after falling victim to political repression for opposing him. Values are not equally shared across the nation, but the people want to preserve their freedom of speech, politics, and travel, and restore what they see as essentially Mongol, their traditional lifestyle.

TRADITIONAL MONGOL VALUES

To show interest in Mongol nationalism and Genghis Khan was a serious political error for much of the twentieth century, the years of communist rule. Yet Mongols have always followed strong leaders. The concept of the supreme leader was reinforced as Stalin rose to power in the USSR and headed the world communist movement. Attitudes toward Mongolia's own "Stalin," Choibalsan, who was the country's supreme ruler from the 1930s to 1952 and who was ultimately responsible for the killing of tens of thousands of people falsely accused of treachery or counter-revolution, still remain ambiguous.

Genghis Khan

The founder of the Mongolian state warned his people
not to forget being Mongols, and this has been a
constant theme of the nationalist agenda. At the birth of
democracy in Mongolia in 1990 Genghis Khan was the
first national hero to be restored and honored. Statues
were erected, books written, films made, and his warrior
image was retained, although his status as a lawmaker
has also been promoted. Usually he is depicted in armor
on horseback, as in the case of the giant statue at Delüün
Boldog, but in the Genghis Khan Square statue he is
enthroned like Abraham Lincoln. His portrait appears
on most Mongolian banknotes. The use of his name for
branding has been banned.

The teachings of Genghis Khan are preserved in the
yasa, a collection of laws and decrees, including taboos
(no washing of the body or clothes in running water,
lest it be polluted), and rules on the family, property,
and inheritance: sentences of death for theft, adultery,
and telling lies, the execution of nobles without shedding
blood. There are collections of Genghis Khan's *yarlik*
(orders) and *bilik* (maxims).

The Spirit World

Like Genghis Khan, the Mongols still believe in the world
of spirits, which, if placated, protect the people and their
herds and flocks. Cairns of stones (*ovoo*), erected at a
crossroads or on a hilltop, are sometimes decorated with
the horns of a sheep, a horse's jaw-bone or skull, and
prayer flags. Travelers may dismount and walk around
it clockwise three times, sprinkle vodka, and pray to the
local spirits, adding a few stones before continuing their
journey. Building of *ovoo* may be linked to the ancient
burial of important persons in high places, and is probably
shamanic, pre-dating Lamaism, which tended to absorb
traditions that it had tried unsuccessfully to stop (see
pages 47–8). Each year the President of Mongolia and his
entourage pay homage to the guardian spirits with special
ceremonies at a number of sacred mountains, including
Burkhan Khaldun at Genghis's birthplace in Khentii, and
Bogd Khan Mountain near Ulan Bator, whose guardian
spirit is a mythological Garuda bird.

Astrology

Many Mongols believe in fortune telling and astrology,
using either the traditional Mongolian lunar astrology
or Western solar astrology, whose charts are published
in popular newspapers and special calendars. They also
believe in the power of numbers (numerology), a feature
of Lamaism. The lunar calendar features twelve animals
and five elements; nine white horse tails make up the
state banner; and the "nines" are the eighty-one (nine
times nine) days of extreme cold usually experienced
in mid-winter. The number 108 (twelve times nine) is
also significant: the number of beads in a rosary, and the
number of stupas in the boundary walls of Erdene Zuu
monastery.

National Symbols
Flag and emblem
The Mongolian flag carries at the hoist the national symbol of independence, a device called the *soyombo* designed by Zanabazar, the first Mongolian Öndör Gegeen. Part of an alphabet he devised, also called *soyombo*, it is said to mean in Sanskrit "self-revealed light." At the center is an *arga bilig* or *yin-yang* symbol, representing the male and female principles (complementary opposites). More obvious symbols are the sun, moon, and a triple flame. A five-pointed star was added in the communist period, but removed in 1992.

When the Great Khural (national assembly) adopted the new constitution in 1992, it also approved a new design for the national emblem, which depicted a mounted herdsman riding toward the sunrise. Most members favored a horse rather than a falcon, the emblem of Genghis Khan. At the center is a stylized yellow wind-horse (*khiimori*) carrying the *soyombo* on its back, flying across "eternal blue heaven" over ranges of rounded green hills. Beneath is a yellow *cakra*, or wheel of the law, like a ship's wheel, with a blue *khadag* (ceremonial scarf) wound through the spokes. Resting on white lotuses, the whole is encircled by a *tümen nasan*, or long-life swastika meander, surmounted by three teardrop gems (*chandmani*) representing the past, present, and future, or perhaps the Buddha, Dharma (teaching), and Sangha (the monk community). The swastika (*khas*) is a Buddhist symbol. It is found as a pattern on the interior walls of the Great Khural, and as a *deel* pattern. Sometimes it is displayed on blue flags at nationalist demonstrations.

Banners

The Great White Banner, symbol of prosperity, strength, and peace, is made of white horsetail hair, and has a three-tongued fire symbol on top of a long pole. It is displayed with eight smaller white banners as its "envoys," at the opening of Naadam, for example (see pages 114–16). When not in use it is displayed on a special stand in the State Palace. The Great Black Banner, symbol of military power, is made of the tail hair of black stallions and has four pendants (representing vigilance for the enemy in the four compass directions), and a spearhead on top. When not on display it is stored at the Ministry of Defense.

Seals

The Khan's seal was inscribed, "By the power of eternal heaven, the conveyed decrees of the Dalai Khan of the Great Mongolian State are to be worshiped and obeyed by all." On appointment the prime minister and ministers are presented with their seal of office in an ornate box on a blue *khadag*, usually by their predecessor. Mongolian offices at all levels still attach great importance to seals (stamps), which are applied in red to all official documents under signature. A monument to the great seal of state stands in the gardens at the northern end of the State Palace.

Family and Clan

The Mongols practice exogamous patrilineage, that is, they marry outside their clan to avoid inbreeding. Most traditional clan names are based on place names. The banning of clan names in the socialist period in 1925 led to confusion and concern. The right to keep family trees and use clan names was restored in the 1990s, and people who didn't know their clan name could choose one. Three-quarters of the population registered their clan name as Borjigon—that of the "golden family" of Genghis.

A husband and wife each retain their own clan name, and the father's clan name is passed on to their children (see Names, page 154). The firstborn son is particularly welcomed as the continuer of the father's clan. He has high standing as the *akh*, or elder brother of the siblings, and is addressed by them and their parents as *ta*, the polite form of the personal pronoun, while younger children are called *chi*, the familiar form. The youngest son is the "guardian of the hearth," and inherits his father's home and possessions.

In modern urban conditions care of the young children of working parents is often in the hands of grandparents, who may live in an adjacent *ger* or share accommodation in the family home. Mongols are loyal to their family and their clan, and have great respect for the wisdom and experience of their elders. It is common for Mongol families to live with three generations in one household, and couples tend to have several children. Partners are loyal to one another whether or not they are married, and some marry only after the birth of their first child. Children are brought up to be self-reliant, travel alone from a young age, and in rural areas are given household responsibilities including the care of young livestock. Adults tend to be independent and individualistic.

Conformity and Individualism

Mongols are law-abiding and accept instructions from officials, including the police—although driving discipline tends to be erratic, if not aggressive, and accidents are commonplace, especially those resulting from drunk driving. The people excel at individual sports, not only traditional ones like wrestling, horse racing, and archery, but also international competitive sports such as shooting, boxing, judo, taekwondo, sumo, and chess. On the other hand there have been few Mongolian successes in international football, basketball, or other team sports.

Individualism plus alcohol can be a potent combination, and Momgol men can be stubborn and argumentative. Fights are not uncommon, even between educated and supposedly responsible people. To seek redress for supposed libel or misrepresentation, government officials, members of the national assembly, and businessmen tend to resort to the courts.

National Pride

Mongolia's majority population are Khalkh Mongols, and their language is by law the standard speech of the whole country. As the majority in the only independent Mongol state, the Khalkh regard themselves as the dominant Mongol tribe, and this has led to differences not only between them and Mongol minorities— particularly the Oirat (western) Mongols—but also Mongols from Inner Mongolia, in China, who are little different ethnically from themselves. This has led to discord between them over who is a "proper" Mongol.

Another aspect of nationalism is defense of the "purity" of the Mongol language in the face of "pollution" by words from foreign languages, particularly English now, although quite a lot of words from Russian and other languages have long been in use. The State Language Council, which monitors such matters, in June 2014 published in several issues of the newspaper *Ödriin Sonin* an alphabetic list of widely used "foreign" words with Mongolian equivalents, inviting readers to supply better alternatives. "It is the precious duty of every Mongol to make our Mongolian language clean and pure," the council said.

Purity
Mongols are quite taken up with the theme of purity in the form of clean lakes, rivers, and streams, stemming from the instructions given them by Genghis Khan not to pollute water sources. This did not reflect any awareness of hygiene, but simple respect for the spirits of nature, preventing illness among the people and their livestock. The idea of pure water has in modern times been extended, with rather less success, to avoiding air pollution by factory chimneys, domestic stoves, and exhaust fumes.

At the same time the Mongols still believe in exogamous marriage and maintaining racial purity, that is, they discourage inbreeding and foreign contamination that would weaken their stock. The population of Mongolia is three million (2015), of neighboring China over 1.4 billion, and of Russia 143 million.

The Group
In addition to the ties of family, clan, and tribe, Mongols remain close to group alliances, formed in their home

province (*aimag*) or locality (*nutag*). There is a verb *nutgarkhakh*, from *nutag*, which means "to favor people from one's own locality." Fellowships at school or in college, including societies and NGOs of alumni and graduates, particularly those who graduated from Russian, American, or British colleges, are popular. These ties are close and important enough in some circumstances for friendship and mutual support to stir suspicions of corruption—nepotism and conflicts of interest in employment, for example.

Patriotism and Politics
During the socialist period patriotism meant brotherhood with the USSR and acceptance of the Kremlin's political and economic leadership. Since 1990 the new patriotism means observing Mongol traditions (wearing the *deel*, the national dress), ceremonial (the nine white banners), allegiance (swearing oaths to the state flag), standing hand on heart for the national anthem, and so on. Patriotism has also been claimed by the Mongolian People's Party as part of its own heritage, as if membership of the MPP were a prerequisite for calling oneself a patriot. Patriots' Day, March 1, marks the anniversary of the founding of the party in 1920.

RELIGION
According to the 2010 national census, half the Mongolian population over the age of fifteen are Buddhists. Having been brought up in an atheistic society, the other half are atheists or agnostics, to whom Buddhism is a tradition rather than a religion. Buddhism displaced the native Mongolian religions, Shamanism and Tengerism, and accommodated those aspects that it

was unable to eradicate completely. It flourished under Manchu rule. Islam in Mongolia is essentially the religion of the Kazakh minority. Christianity was spread among the Mongols by missionaries in the nineteenth century, banned for most of the twentieth century, and relaunched after the birth of democracy in 1990.

A 2015 survey of religious organizations in Ulan Bator revealed the existence of 234 active registered places of worship, of which 61.3 percent were Christian (seven Catholic) and 28.5 percent Buddhist, plus twenty-two shamanic centers. Two-thirds of the total were in the capital's *ger* districts.

Buddhism

Most Mongolian Buddhists are followers of the Dalai Lama's Gelugpa, or "yellow hat" order, often called Lamaists, whose Mahayana ("great vehicle") doctrine

offers easy and certain universal salvation through a system combining theism and mysticism. The Gelugpa headquarters in Mongolia is Ulan Bator's Gandan monastery, named after the Gandan ("paradise") monastery near Lhasa. The Abbot of Gandan, Khamba Lama Choijamts, is the leader of Mongolia's Buddhists. The current Dalai Lama, the fourteenth, has visited Mongolia several times; the thirteenth fled to Mongolia when British troops invaded Tibet in 1904 and stayed until 1906.

Sonom Darje, recognized by the Dalai Lama as the reincarnation of the eighth Javzandamba, who as Bogd

Khan (head of state) ruled Mongolia 1911–24, was born near Lhasa in 1932 and studied at Drepung, but fled Tibet to India in 1961 and made his way to Dharamsala, to join the Dalai Lama in exile. He first visited Ulan Bator briefly in 1999, and was enthroned at Erdene Zuu monastery as the ninth Öndör Gegeen and leader of Mongolia's Buddhists. He went back to Dharamsala, returned to Mongolia permanently in 2009, took Mongolian citizenship, but died in 2012. Abbot Choijamts was reinstated as leader of Mongolia's Buddhists. There has been much speculation about the search for a new incarnation of the Bogd Gegeen (Öndör Gegeen), as well as whether the Dalai Lama might be reincarnated in Mongolia.

The Gelugpas have predominated in Mongolia since Altan Khan converted to the "yellow" faith after meeting its Tibetan leader in 1578 and naming him as Dalai Lama. The first Öndör Gegeen, Zanabazar (1635–1723), son of the Khalkh Tüsheet Khan Gombodorj, was recognized as the incarnation of a Tibetan scholar, Taranatha, incarnated from a line of earlier Tibetan "reverend holinesses" (Javzandamba) and enthroned in the yellow hare year (1639–40). He studied in Tibet under the fifth Dalai Lama. It was Zanabazar who advised the Khalkh Mongols, after they were attacked by the Oirats, to form an alliance with the Manchus (see page 23).

Möngke, the fourth Great Khan, patronized the Karmapa, or "black hat" order, and Kublai, the fifth Great Khan, favored the Sakya, a "red hat" school. Today, Mongolian followers of the "red hats" and "black hats" have their own monasteries, including the Sakya Namdoldechin in the Ulan Bator suburbs. Mongolian Buddhists were persecuted in the 1930s, and from the 1940s until the democratic revolution in 1990 only Gandan monastery functioned, as a showpiece to impress Buddhists from other Asian countries, and later as a tourist attraction.

Shamanism

It was estimated in 2010 that there are more than 55,000 Mongolian believers in shamanism. The word "shaman" comes from a Siberian tribal language and denotes a person who has access to the spirit world and is empowered by it to cure illness and give guidance. Shamanism is related to local folk religion such as veneration of fire, ancestor worship, and mountain spirits. A shaman has distinctive clothing and equipment, in particular a drum for summoning the spirits, and communicates in a state of ecstasy with "white" (good) spirits or "black" (malevolent) ones. The shaman practices divination and exorcism, but there are no birth, marriage, or death rituals. With the flourishing of Lamaism, shamanism camouflaged itself with Lamaist symbols and they peacefully coexisted. Under Soviet rule shamans were persecuted. In February 2015 dozens of shamans gathered in Genghis Khan Square to pray to the spirits of Noyon Uul, an important Hun burial site near Züünkharaa, to protect it from officials turning the nearby Gatsuurt gold mine into a "strategic" deposit.

Tengerism

Belief in a heavenly power, "eternal blue heaven" (*mönkh khökh tenger*), to which all other powers are subject, has been part of the pattern of belief since the times of Genghis Khan, the original "blue skies thinker." He believed that he had been designated by "eternal heaven" to rule the world. The cult of ancestor worship extended to him, although today the only extant shrine for sacrifices to Genghis is at Ezen Khoroo in Ordos, Inner Mongolia. There is an Eternal Blue Heaven Believers' Association headed by a "heavenly father" in Ulan Bator.

Islam

Mongolian Muslims number just over 57,000 (2010), mostly Sunni Mongol Kazakhs. There are twenty or so congregations and a similar number of clergy, mostly in western provinces of Mongolia (Bayan-Ölgii and Khovd), and in population centers such as Ulan Bator and Darkhan. There has long been talk of building a mosque and Kazakh cultural center near Ulan Bator railway station. The mosques in western Mongolia are community centers with prayer-halls. The Chief Imam is resident in Ölgii. Since 1990 Mongol Kazakhs have been free to travel abroad, and each year a few join the Hajj. The new year (Nauryz) is celebrated in Kazakh-inhabited areas (see Public Holidays).

Christianity

There are about 42,000 Mongolian Christians, and 151 congregations, the majority in Ulan Bator (2010). The Catholic mission is represented by an apostolic prefect and there is a cathedral, of St. Peter and St. Paul. The Russian Orthodox community in Ulan Bator is centered on the rebuilt Holy Trinity church, which before 1921 served the Russian trading community. The Association of Mongolian Protestants, the Evangelical Alliance, and the Baptists established themselves in Ulan Bator after 1990. The authorities became concerned about Christian missionary activities in Mongolia, and the Law on the Separation of State and Religion was initially used to discourage them; later the authorities were prevailed upon to allow them as part of the democratic process, but some Mongols still dislike foreign missionary activity. Mormons and Seventh-Day Adventists are also active.

There is quite a long history of Christian outreach to the Mongols. In the medieval period there were several papal missions to the Khan's capital, although they might be considered more political than religious. In the nineteenth century missionaries of the Moravian Church were active in the Mongol lands. There are several translations into Mongol of the Old and New Testaments of the Bible, including publications of the British and Foreign Bible Society.

POSITION AND POWER

The leading figure in any political party or business is the head, boss, or chairman (*darga*, a word apparently related to the Persian *daroga* and part of the vocabulary of empire). The words for president and prime minister, posts introduced in Mongolia in the 1990s, are both based on the word *yörönkhii*, meaning chief of things generally. The top *darga* in Mongolia is the chairman (speaker) of the Great Khural. The term secretary also includes the word *darga*, the "boss of the exact writing," whether this is an office worker or the leader of a political party or trade union. Rank and hierarchy are structurally defined, and posts in the civil service are graded.

The roles of president, speaker, and prime minister are described in the Constitution and in laws drawn up on its basis. Politicians can increase their popularity by helping to run sports such as horse racing or wrestling, or working with philanthropic organizations helping the disabled, homeless, etc. A good many politicians have accumulated, through private business and property ownership, considerable wealth, which is on public display in their annual income returns. From time to time the press reports that high-ranking leaders (ex-President Enkhbayar is an example) have been imprisoned or fined for fraud or bribery. High-ranking officials sometimes give way to their sense of entitlement and may take advantage to display their position of power.

The bosses know what the problems are and what to do, and they know that everyone else is wrong. Denigrating people and casting aspersions are commonplace. Generally speaking Mongols are submissive in their attitude toward their bosses and the authorities—part of the national inheritance from the period of Soviet control. The popular press publicizes issues of gross negligence and inefficiency.

MEN

Mongolia is not a particularly macho society, but some manly values are admired, including physical strength, in terms of the national sport of traditional Mongolian wrestling, free-style wrestling, judo, and sumo, as well as bodybuilding. In recent years Mongolia has produced several world sumo champions. Leaders display what physical skills they can, riding horses and shooting arrows from a traditional wooden bow in Naadam competitions (see page 66), as President Elbegdorj does, or climbing high mountains as ex-President Enkhbayar has done. Men like to wear the traditional *deel* and show off the silver buckles, knives, and accessories on their belts, in the Genghis Khan tradition, they think. They are fond of wearing both traditional and modern headgear. There is strong competition to gain entry to the horse-trainers' association, and the Ulan Bator golf club.

However, irritation and drunkenness can inflame the warrior spirit, and differences of opinion can lead to fights causing injury. Drunkenness is the cause of many deaths on the roads, and of violence in the home. On average about three hundred people a year are murdered, between 60 and 80 percent of them victims of domestic violence. After an increase in reported crime in 2014, the focus of the spring 2015 anti-crime campaign has been on stopping child trafficking and domestic violence.

WOMEN

It was customary for the voice of women to be heard in matters of importance. Urged by his wife Börte, Genghis Khan decided to break his alliance with Jamukha and suppress the shaman Kököchü. There are examples of Mongol women in the past having held positions of high status, influence, and responsibility, in particular the widows of some of the Great Khans, who ruled the empire for interregnums of several years. Women enjoy extensive equality with men, reflecting perhaps the sharing of duties in the traditional herding household.

During the Soviet period equality of men and women was promoted as part of communist doctrine, that is, through the formation of the Mongolian Women's Committee, founded by the MPRP in 1924, which until

1990 was the only official women's political organization. Yanjmaa, widow of the revolutionary hero Sükhbaatar, held honorary posts in the political hierarchy for many years after her husband's death. When Tsedenbal was head of state (1974–84) his Russian wife Anastasia, a domineering figure, apparently involved herself much more in political life than the Politburo liked. Although the membership of the Great Khural often exceeded two hundred deputies, including a regular proportion of women heroes of labor and champion milkmaids, few rose to the highest party and state ranks.

After 1990, the reformed political parties set up their own women's organizations, including the MPRP's Democratic Socialist Women's Organization, and the DP's Democratic Women's Association. Several women's voluntary bodies, associations, and NGOs have emerged. However, the proportion of women nominated by political parties to stand for election remains small. The 2012 election saw only eleven women elected among the seventy-six members of the Great Khural. While women constitute 60 percent of graduates in Mongolia, only 30 percent of middle managers and 15 percent of top managers are women.

With the inauguration of the post of president came the new role of "first lady." Modest in their public image, presidents' wives have tended to become involved in charity activities, care for disabled children, and the like. A rare example of a woman in a position of popular leadership is Oyuun, sister of the minister and leading democrat Zorig who was murdered in 1998. She founded a political party to fight for justice in his name called Civil Courage (*irgenii zorig*) of which she remains leader. She has been elected to the Great Khural several times, served as Minister of Foreign Affairs 2007–8, and was Minister of the Environment 2012–14.

ATTITUDES TOWARD EDUCATION

Mongols are eager for education, and there are high levels of literacy across the board. A century ago there were no schools in Mongolia. Boys could become novices (lamas) in monasteries and learn to read Buddhist texts in Tibetan. If they were lucky and gifted they might be taken on for training as clerks in a local government office. Generally clerks were taught to read Mongolian, and, if they showed promise, to write it too—a separate qualification. A government-run primary school opened in Ulan Bator in 1921, and a secondary school in 1923, but there were few teachers. The Ministry of Education was established in 1924. According to an official history, there were only ten thousand or so literates in 1926. A "cultural offensive" was launched in 1930 to liquidate illiteracy by replacing the classical *uigarjin* script of Genghis Khan with a Latin alphabet, but this was replaced by a Cyrillic alphabet in 1940. Universal compulsory education of school-age children was introduced in 1955.

Youth literacy is now 96 percent, and Mongolia has 752 general education schools, where the pupil–teacher ratio averages 18.3. The National University of Mongolia opened in 1942, and there are now ten universities, of which eight are privately funded. Hundreds of Mongolian students are studying at universities abroad. Under a scheme called Beehive, the government encourages young people studying abroad to come back to Mongolia after graduating, so that the country benefits from their education and skills. The ministry responsible for education also supervises culture and science, meaning museums, libraries, and cinemas as well as schools, universities, research institutes, and the Academy of Sciences. (See also pages 96–7).

ATTITUDES TOWARD WORK

The Western work ethic doesn't apply to traditional Mongolian society. Riding around their herds all day, the herdsmen seem lazy and unproductive, but in reality animal care in all hours, weathers, and seasons is vital to the economy, and life in rural areas remains hard and living conditions difficult. Herdsmen like the freedom of the traditional way of life, and these days increasingly enjoy some of the home comforts of their urban relatives, especially mains electricity and TV. However, some of the younger generation give up herding and move to the towns, seeking better-paid work and more excitement.

It was not until large-scale Soviet investment from the 1950s that industrial output increased substantially. The army was trained as a construction force. The ruling political party encouraged pride in the new working class, and productivity was encouraged through various incentive schemes, which may have compensated to some extent for low wages and poor housing. The workforce grew and diversified, as did the bureaucracy of officials and managers. Factory workers and office staff still tend to absent themselves during working hours to attend to personal matters such as dental appointments, or shopping, a legacy of the need to circumvent the inflexibility of socialist times.

Education abroad and exposure of government officials and business leaders to Western practices has revolutionized business in Mongolia. Better working conditions and wages have boosted regular work attendance and reduced casual absenteeism. Clocking in and improved punctuality have ensured smoother production in factories and customer service in shops and offices and enhanced the productiveness of business conferences. The introduction of modern machinery and safety procedures, protective clothing, and helmets has raised morale and productivity.

The workforce is mostly well trained and industrious. Big foreign mining companies still employ relatively

"Mongolizing" the Job

During the period of "building socialism" in Mongolia in the 1960s and '70s there were periods of shortages when the planned economy required workers to "make do and mend" and vehicle drivers, for example, to be sparing with fuel and lubricants, and repair their own punctures. In the event of breakdowns workers often had to use their wits. Quite often the correct tools or equipment were unavailable for repairs and the work was badly done, for example by using a hammer when a wrench was needed. This was known as "mongolizing" the job—doing it in the Mongol way (*mongolchlokh*), or improvising.

These days, in the depths of winter, motor vehicles need to be parked overnight in heated premises to prevent engines from freezing up. In the country there might be no heated place available. The solution to this familiar problem? In the morning light a fire under the cylinder block!

large numbers of foreign workers to operate complex and expensive machinery while training Mongolian workers on the job. People like to set up companies so they can be their own boss and diversify their field of operation, but the number of small companies closing within a year of start-up is relatively large. The main growth area is retail trade, employing 156,000 of the workforce, while mining employs only 50,000 (2013). Market gardening is another growth area that shows independence and enterprise.

chapter three

CUSTOMS & TRADITIONS

NATIONAL DRESS

The *deel* is a long gown, worn by both sexes. Women wore it traditionally without a sash or belt, and the Mongol word for a woman is *büsgüi*, that is, "beltless." Today many women do add a belt. The *deel* has a high collar and buttons up at the right shoulder. In rural areas it is in everyday use; city dwellers usually wear European dress.

For summer the *deel* is of cotton or patterned Chinese silk, worn by men with a sash of contrasting color, or a heavy leather belt with silver buckles, and traditionally a sheath knife with chopstick holder. The best silk *deels* are reserved for holidays or festive occasions. The winter *deel*

is lined with padding or fur. A practical feature is long sleeves that cover the hands, keeping them warm but leaving the fingers free.

Men wear leather boots (*gutal*), incised with traditional patterns and painted, which have turned-up toes to protect the feet from trampling by animals, and stout socks made of embroidered felt.

In the Manchu Empire hats were an important symbol of a man's rank and status. On top they had "buttons" of semi-precious

stones showing the wearer's rank. In Qing times winter hats were often made of animal skin and had a circular brim, while conical summer hats were made of bamboo strips. Winter hats are still made of fur, often a whole fox, with tail.

During the socialist period most men not in uniform wore a flat cap indicating their "working-class" origin, while officials adopted Soviet suits and trilby hats. These days traditional generals' hats (*janjin malgai*) with earflaps and topped with a small colored ball are worn mostly by wrestlers, with ribbons to show their ranking. Guards of honor wear helmets and uniforms based on dress from the revolutionary period, including sabers.

Despite the encouragement of traditional dress since 1990, broad-brimmed "bush" hats and Stetsons have become popular with men. Often worn indoors by both men and women, hats are special and personal, and people don't usually exchange headgear or touch the hats of others.

THE *GER*

More than half the population of Mongolia live in a
traditional *ger,* or round tent (Russian: *yurta*), with wall
sections (*khana*) of flexible wooden latticework. At the
center of the *ger* stands a stove for cooking and heating.
The chimney protrudes through a hole in the roof
formed by a circular wooden frame supported on two
stout vertical poles, with a roof flap to let in the light. The
roof is supported on thinner poles resting like the spokes
of a wheel on top of the lattice. The whole is covered with
felt for warmth and canvas to keep the rain out, roped
together and weighted to resist the wind. Large items
such as the stove, beds, and chests, are placed inside the
lattice before enclosure. The woodwork is usually painted
orange and decorated with traditional patterns.

The *ger* is always pitched with the painted wooden
door facing south. Sunlight entering through the roof
frame, as observed from inside the *ger*, traces a path
across the floor and walls, from which the passage of
time can be gauged. The names of the twelve astrological
animals (see The Mongolian Calendar, on page 64) are
also used for the hours of the day and night. Traditional
Mongol "hours" are equal to two European hours, and

are measured not from the European hour but from forty minutes past the hour. The wooden door opens outward, and visitors should not step on the threshold, as this is thought to bring bad luck.

Internally the *ger* is divided into the northern quadrant, where religious images and family photos are displayed on a cupboard, and the senior man and honored guests sit on stools at a low wooden table where food and drink are served. The western quadrant, the man's, is where the herdsman keeps his saddle and tack and where the koumiss (*airag*) bag of mare's milk is hung to ferment. The eastern quadrant, the woman's, is where cooking utensils and household effects are stored. Next to the stove on the door side is the fuel box, storing dried animal dung. Water is brought from a local spring or river. Some *gers* have a dry latrine some distance away, in a tall wooden cupboard. Otherwise people answer nature's call out in the open air, behind a suitable bush or rock if available.

The *ger* is the hemispherical heart of the Mongols' concentric world. The woman's responsibilities range beyond domestic matters and raising the children to the milking of animals and making of cheeses, and the care of newborn lambs and kids, which are kept close to the

ger, or inside. The horses in use are tied nearby. The man's responsibilities extend over the broader surrounding area, where the horses and cattle roam, but must be kept moving from one pasture to another and ensured a water supply. Depending on conditions, he decides when to pack everything up and move on to a new area of grazing.

THE MONGOLIAN CALENDAR

The Mongolian lunar calendar is based on cycles of twelve years, named tiger, hare, dragon, snake, horse, sheep, monkey, chicken, dog, pig, mouse, and ox. According to legend, when God thought up the animal year cycle, he decided to include the first twelve animals he would see the next day. However, the camel and the mouse turned up together, so God told them that the winner would be the first to see the next sunrise. The camel ran up a hill and faced east, but the mouse, which had mounted the camel's back, faced west. From the top of a hump (Mongolian camels have two) the mouse saw sunlight fall on distant mountains, and won the contest. That is how the mouse, and not the camel, came to be one of the animals of the lunar calendar.

The animal years are alternately male and female, and combine with five elements—wood, fire, earth, iron, and water—represented by the colors blue, red, yellow, white, and black respectively. The five elements (colors) apply for two-year periods, and in combination with the twelve animal years create a cycle of sixty years (a *jaran*, or "Buddhist century") in which each year is uniquely named. The current *jaran*, the seventeenth, began in 1987. The lunar year 2014 is the wooden (blue) horse (stallion) year, and 2015 the wooden (blue) sheep (ewe) year, to be followed by the fire (red) monkey year in 2016. The lunar months are called, for example, "first summer month," "third winter month," and so on, or may be named after the twelve animals. Tsagaan Sar and Genghis Khan's anniversary are celebrated according to the lunar calendar, but the other anniversaries follow the Western solar calendar, which is in general use, the months simply being numbered from first to twelfth.

PUBLIC HOLIDAYS
On these days offices and shops are closed, but stalls sell food and drink at the Naadam stadium. Special arrangements are in force for public transport, car parking, and so forth.

January 1: New Year's Day
First celebrated in 1947. A "new year's tree" is set up in Genghis Khan Square in December, and the "Old Man of Winter" (*övliin övgön*) distributes gifts to children. A new tradition is catching on for Ulan Bator inhabitants: a trip to the country to see the first sunrise of the year. The greeting is: "*Shine ony bayaryn mend khürgeye!*" "Wishing you a happy new year!"

Tsagaan Sar, the Mongolian Lunar New Year

A major three-day holiday beginning on the first day (*shiniin neg*) of the lunar new year ("white moon"), at the end of January or beginning of February. It is usually celebrated in Mongolia and China on the same day, unless their astrologers disagree about leap months. The greeting is: "*Sar shinedee saikhan shineleerei!*" "Have a nice first of the month!"

Preparations for this most important annual festival include cleaning and tidying the home, and the purchase of gifts and traditional foods, ranging from fried pastries (*boov*) to a whole fat-tailed sheep (*uuts*).

March 8: International Women's Day

Marked in Mongolia as UN Day for Women's Rights and World Peace from 1977, subsequently Women's Rights Protection Day. Flowers are given to women on this day.

June 1: Mother and Child Day

Established in 1949 by the Women's International Democratic Federation, now celebrated as International Day for Protection of Children. Special events are laid on at the Children's Park in Ulan Bator and elsewhere.

July 11–13: Naadam

The traditional sports festival takes place in Ulan Bator, with mounted soldiers in historic uniform, dancers and musicians in national dress, wrestling, archery, and horse racing in the countryside. (See also page 114.)

From the 1950s, the anniversary of the Mongolian 1921 revolution and the capital's liberation was marked with military parades and workers' demonstrations in Sükhbaatar Square on July 11, but this was abandoned after 1993.

TSAGAAN SAR

Eating and drinking are an important part of the celebrations. The eve of moonrise of the new lunar year is called *bitüün*, and people go home early from work. Schools close, most offices and businesses close for three days, and public transport runs restricted services. Emergency services, hospitals, and pharmacies remain open.

On the first day of the lunar new year everyone puts on their best clothes to visit nearby family and friends and pass on new-year greetings As a mark of respect, younger people place their hands beneath the elbows of their elders, as if to lift them up (*zolgokh*), exchanging *khadags* (ceremonial blue silk scarves), and taking snuff from each other's snuff bottles. When passing vodka, a snuff bottle, food, or tea to guests, or receiving them, the givers and receivers support their own right arm at the elbow with the left hand.

The president's first duty on lunar New Year's Day is to pay homage to Genghis Khan in Genghis Khan Square. He then returns to the State Palace where he bows to the Mongolian state emblem (the flying horse) and the white horsetail banners. The president meets the national assembly speaker and the prime minister, all wearing *deels* and fur hats, to perform traditional ceremonial greetings from armchairs in the State Palace's reception *ger*. The tables are piled up with stacks of *boov*, cheeses, and sweets, together with giant bowls of koumiss. There is musical accompaniment from a horse-head fiddle (*morin khuur*; see page 106), and the president delivers a new-year message to the nation on TV.

National Pride Day (Mongol Bakharkhlyn Ödör)
Genghis Khan's birthday is celebrated on the first day
of the first winter month of the lunar calendar. There
are ceremonies of raising the state flag and installing
the Nine White Banners, followed by presentations of
the Order of Genghis Khan. In the past Genghis Khan's
birthday was marked on May 31, and was not a holiday.

**November 26: Republic Day (Bügd Nairamdakh Uls
Tunkhaglasyn Oin Bayaryn Odor)**
This day marks the anniversary of the adoption of the
first constitution and the proclamation of the MPR in
1924. Some people call it Independence Day. A survival
from the communist past, before the Independence and
Genghis Khan anniversaries were established, today it is
simply an opportunity to enjoy a day off.

**December 29: National Freedom and Independence
Anniversary (Mongol, Uls Ündesnii Erkh Chölöö,
Tusgaar Togtnoliin Oi)**
This day marks the anniversary of the declaration of
Mongolian independence on the fall of Qing rule in 1911
(celebrated for the first time in 2007). The leaders hold

a ceremony at the state seal monument in the gardens north of the State Palace in Ulan Bator. During the 2013 anniversary the foundations of a memorial to the Bogd Khan were laid in Independence Square.

Nauryz
Although it is not a national holiday, the spring equinox festival marking the new year (March 22) of the Kazakhs and some other Central Asian peoples is celebrated in Mongolian Kazakh communities. The Mongol president usually issues a message of greetings: "*Nauryz meiramy kütti bolsyn!*" "Have a happy Nauryz!" In 2015 he said it would be nice if the festival could be celebrated "without drunkenness and vodka." This ancient festival, which is of Iranian origin (*nowruz*, new day or new light), seems to have been banned in 1926 and revived in 1990. The Mongols call it the "sun festival" (*narny bayar*).

THE SPOKEN WORD
Mongolian bards committed to memory epics of colossal length. There is strong belief in the magical power of the spoken word, emanating from the prehistoric past: benedictions on birth or marriage, departure on a journey, or acquisition of a new *ger*, blessings of newborn babies and animals, or of new tools and weapons. There are taboos associated with the invocation of mountain spirits, which are usually avoided, and certain words, such as "wolf."

The modern versions of these practices are the swearing of oaths of allegiance to the state flag by soldiers and civil servants, state ceremonies with the nine white horsetail banners attended by the president, and military parades with the army's black horsetail banner.

Proverbs

One may gauge something of traditional Mongol attitudes from proverbs and sayings. Some seem familiar, like the Mongolian equivalents of "Actions speak louder than words" and "Nothing ventured, nothing gained." The Mongolian for "No smoke without fire" is "Where would the magpie sit if the *ovoo* had not been built?"

Other sayings relate to particularly Mongol circumstances: "Having no debt is wealth and no illness happiness." "Add salt till it dissolves, do the work till it's finished." "A careless word cannot be taken back, a lost gelding cannot be recovered." "High mountains are windy, old people are fussy." "Close to vodka there are many friends."

One saying is used quite a lot in the current business scene: "Dividing the skin before killing the bear." In other words, planning how to spend the money before it's been earned. There is also the saying "Many people put their fingers in a dead bear's mouth," that is, when it's safe to do so. Animals often feature in folktales and proverbs. If something is done on the sly, it is "like a wolf in the rain, or a crow in the dark." "Out of the frying pan into the fire" is "Out of the wolf's mouth into the tiger's."

BIRTH AND INFANCY

It is thought to be unlucky to make special preparations for a birth. A baby is considered to be a year old when it is born. Three or seven days after birth the close family wash the baby and give him or her a name, which a lama may be invited to confer, but more usually the father or grandparents. Family members bring presents of money, clothes, toys, or, in rural areas, a knife, a bow and arrows, a saddle, or a sheep.

For boys at the age of three or five, and girls aged two or four, on an auspicious day family and friends hold a formal first hair-cutting ceremony. The child is seated in the place of honor at the back of the *ger* and a man born in the same animal year is the first to cut the child's hair, followed by the eldest. The child receives greetings of goodwill and long life, and goes around with a tray, scissors, and a *khadag*—a ceremonial blue silk scarf, into which a religious symbol may have been woven. Each guest cuts some hair and places it on the tray with gifts. The cut hair is wrapped in the *khadag* and stored away by the family, and any hair remaining on the child's head may be shaved off. The child is encouraged to behave solemnly during the proceedings, even if not always entirely happy.

TRADITIONAL WEDDINGS

Betrothals used to be arranged before the children were old enough to marry. Men usually married at odd-numbered ages, girls at sixteen or seventeen. The father would look out for a bride for his son as he grew up and, when he found a suitable candidate, send a matchmaker to the girl's parents. The matchmaker took a *khadag* and gifts. If they were accepted, the boy's parents visited the girl's parents to discuss the dowry. If all went well and the dowry (usually livestock) was acceptable, the boy's parents agreed to provide a *ger* and furniture, and the girl's parents a trousseau, including household goods. A lama would choose an astrologically propitious day for the wedding. The day before the wedding the boy set up his own *ger* on the eastern side of his father's, then with his parents visited the bride and her parents to bow to their hearth. The father of the bride would give the boy an arrow as a

symbol of headship of the future family. The bride's
family then took the dowry to the boy's *ger*.

At dawn on the wedding day the groom, smartly
dressed and with a bow and arrows, accompanied by
five or seven young men, took a saddled horse for the
bride to her parents' *ger*. When they arrived there was
a mock struggle, as if the boy were seizing the girl by
force, and the womenfolk would pretend to prevent
this. The boy and girl mounted the horse together, rode
three times round her parents' *ger*, then set off for the
boy's *ger*. Two fires were lit, so that the bride and groom
might be "cleansed" by passing between them. The bride's
hair was redone in married style, according to tribal
custom—for Khalkh women the two braids were combed
into distinctive flat "horns" clasped with silver and coral
ornaments and threaded through tubular silver "hair
cases"—and the jewelry of a married woman was put on.
The bride then entered the boy's parents' *ger* and bowed
to the family hearth and images and to the boy's family.
The groom lit the stove in his *ger* for the first time, and
the bride made tea for her in-laws and guests. This was
often followed by a drunken feast with verbal jousting and
sometimes coarse exchanges between spokesmen for the

groom and bride. On the following day the bride was taken to visit the groom's relatives. From then on she had to obey her mother-in-law.

Genghis Khan had a senior wife (*ikh ekhner*), several junior ones (*baga ekhner*), and concubines— usually the wives and daughters of defeated enemies—but only the children of the senior

wife could succeed. A modern wedding may be a grand affair, with bridesmaids, tuxedos, and bow ties, celebrated at the Wedding Palace in Ulan Bator with a banquet at a hotel or restaurant, or a simple signing ceremony at the local register office, followed by a party with families and friends. Honeymoon trips abroad have become fashionable.

MOURNING AND REMEMBRANCE

Noble families had their own burial grounds, and might be buried secretly, in a wooden coffin, with armor, clothing, concubines, and servants. High lamas were embalmed and sometimes put on display in temples in ceremonial dress. Before burial became the rule, the poor would leave their deceased relatives in the steppe, "a mountain at the head and running water at the feet." The corpse was left for dogs, wild animals, and birds to consume, a practice known as "sky burial," the ideal of selflessness. Mongolian dogs were fierce and dangerous, even in towns. The communist authorities banned sky burial. It was legalized in 1990 as "traditional," if no longer popular.

In modern times crematoria have been operating in Ulan Bator, but two-thirds of the dead are buried in cemeteries. The hearse may be a truck, the coffin loaded in the back, together with mourners and a large portrait of the deceased. The coffin is open during the funeral for last farewells and the placing of personal items by the family with the deceased, then closed for burial. Funerals are held on odd days of the week, but not Sundays. On the forty-ninth day memorial prayers are said and the grave visited, followed by a meatless meal. So that the spirit may be reincarnated, families traditionally do not visit the grave for three years.

Traditional Rites
The dying used to be left to concentrate their thoughts on Buddha, free of earthly problems, and mourning and crying were considered improper. After death the deceased was neither moved nor touched while the contents of the *ger* were removed. The deceased was then laid out, head resting in the palm of the right hand, the left arm straight beside the body, the left leg bent at the knee, the right leg straight. The face was covered with a *khadag*. Oil lamps were lit, the door and roof hole of the *ger* closed. After two days and nights prayers were said for the soul to go to paradise.

According to the date and time of death by the lunar calendar, lamas set a suitable date and place for burial and a person was chosen to "touch" the corpse. The day before burial the corpse was wrapped in a white sheet and placed in a white sack with aromatic herbs. On the day of burial a cart or riding animal was brought, and the chosen person, with prayers written on his hands, entered the *ger*, took up the corpse and placed it on the cart, horse, or camel. Led by a man on a white horse, the procession headed for the chosen place of burial. The grave was marked out and dug, and food, drink, *khadags*, and coins were placed there. The head of the deceased rested on a white stone, and the grave was sprinkled with grain. The mourners would leave the grave by a different route, without looking back. On returning home they cleansed themselves by walking between two fires.

The mourners gathered for a wake (no alcohol) at the *ger*, which had been moved to a new site. On the following days the family went to the local temple to pray. On the twenty-first day after the funeral a painting or figure of the deity most admired by the deceased was made, a bowl of rice placed on the grave, and vodka sprinkled over it.

Cemeteries and Memorials
Since 1990 several secret mass graves have been discovered, containing the remains of people (usually lamas) falsely accused of treason and shot during the 1930s. In such cases, after forensic examination to establish their identity, if possible, the remains are usually cremated and the ashes placed in a suitable memorial stupa. Care is taken to preserve the memory of such victims of political repression, and to ensure that their children and other relatives receive the appropriate compensation under current

legislation. There is a memorial to the "victims of political repression" in Ulan Bator, and the house of the executed former Prime Minister Genden serves as a museum and archive.

Before the 1921 revolution most statues were of the Buddha and other religious subjects in temples. Until 1990 the people commemorated were either communist leaders such as Lenin and Stalin, or "heroic" local soldiers like Sükhbaatar, diligent workers and anti-Manchu rebels. After the Second World War busts and statues of "socialist heroes" multiplied, ranging from General Zhukov to Prime Minister Tsedenbal. Following the Soviet example of the Lenin mausoleum outside the Kremlin, the Mongols built a mausoleum for Sükhbaatar and Choibalsan in front of the State Palace (government house) on Sükhbaatar Square, as it was then called, in Ulan Bator. Standing on the mausoleum's balcony, the country's communist leaders took the salute from marching soldiers and banner-waving workers on May Day and November 7, the anniversary of the Russian October Revolution, as well as Mongolian Revolution Day, July 11. The mausoleum was demolished to make way for the Genghis Khan statue in what is now Genghis Khan Square.

The national cemetery for the burial of political leaders and other distinguished people is at Altan Ölgii, in Ulan Bator, where a new mausoleum for Sükhbaatar and Choibalsan was built in 2005, fenced and guarded. Modern cemeteries sometimes have elaborate graves and tombstones, with model airplanes for dead pilots, or car engine cooling fans spinning in the wind as "prayer flags." Old cemeteries, with grave markers of single stones inscribed in *uigarjin*, are often in poor shape. Sometimes graves are opened by robbers, others disturbed by people needing somewhere to pitch their *ger*.

Despite the democratic reevaluation of the communist purges, a statue of the revolutionary leader Choibalsan, who became Mongolia's dictator in the 1930s, still stands outside the National University. His successor, Tsedenbal, "Mongolia's Brezhnev," had his bust put up in his home in Uvs province in the 1970s, and more recently, after attempts by his relatives and followers to rehabilitate him,

a statue was unveiled opposite the Drama Theater. The people's renewed interest in the prerevolutionary history of their country has stimulated a number of previously forbidden monumental subjects, including Khanddorj, the foreign minister in the Bogd Khan's first government, and Ivan Korostovets, the Imperial Russian envoy to the Bogd Khan.

chapter four

MAKING FRIENDS

ATTITUDES TOWARD FOREIGNERS

From 1207 the expansion of Genghis Khan's Mongol state brought the Mongols into conflict with neighboring nations in what is now northern China, including the Tangut (Xixia), Jurchen (Jin), and Qidan (Western Liao). Despite the Chinese names and reign titles from Chinese records, these were mixed tribal and settled peoples of Mongol, Turkish, or Manchu origin. Not being kin of the Mongols, they were slaughtered in great numbers as Genghis Khan's empire began to grow "under the power of eternal heaven." The Mongol armies invaded Turkestan, and conquered Uighur, Arab, and Persian peoples of Khwarazm.

After the first Mongol incursion into Russian territory (1223) and the death of Genghis Khan (1227), during the conquest of North China (Song), the Great Khan Ögedei was encouraged by his adviser, Yelü Chucai, to tax the civil population rather than exterminate it. Yelü Chucai, who had served the Jin and interpreted omens for Genghis Khan, was a believer in Confucianism and introduced reforms to Mongolian administration, separating the civil and military authorities and setting low tax rates. Administration of the regions of the Mongol Empire generally was supervised by officials brought in from elsewhere. To preserve Mongol state security, local officials were not allowed to learn the Mongol language.

After the disintegration of their empire the homeland of the Mongols came under the control of the Manchu (Qing), and they were treated as a subject people. The powers of the Mongol chiefs were eroded, and the Mongols understandably resented the intrusion of foreign customs and practices. Their relief at the fall of the Qing and the declaration of independence in 1911 was overtaken by dismay at the invasion of the Republic of China army. Their relief at the withdrawal of Chinese troops and the victory of the Mongolian revolutionary forces with Soviet military support was soon tempered by the realization that imposition of communist theories would fundamentally change everything, destroy their traditional Buddhist faith, and divide their small nation. In the 1960s, under Soviet influence, the Mongols were encouraged to fear China.

The birth of democracy in Mongolia in 1990 gave the Mongols many freedoms they had dreamed of, Western ideas they had heard of but not experienced, and traditional ideas they could revert to. The older generation still liked the idea of "fraternal friendship" with Russia, but the younger generation wanted to see things for itself, and readily accepted the consumer boom created by imports of Chinese goods. They were free to travel abroad, and to meet and make friends with foreigners who had not been citizens of the socialist world like them. They have high expectations of such contacts.

The "Eternal Neighbors"

After visits to Mongolia in 2014 by Russia's President Putin and China's Chairman Xi, Mongolian President Elbegdorj felt obliged to say that Mongolia was "lucky to live between two great powers as its eternal neighbors." His aim was to detract from a recent anti-Chinese outburst on TV by a member of the Great Khural (national assembly), who had claimed incorrectly that the building of Chinese-gauge railway lines in Mongolia, to link the Tavan Tolgoi coal deposit with the Chinese railway system, would enable Chinese workers to obtain land and property in Mongolia illegally. This claim was said to have stirred discontent and provoked anti-Chinese sentiment.

Genghis Khan's conquest of Russia, together with the growth of Great Russian nationalism and the power of the Russian Orthodox Church, have left some bitterness between Russians and Mongols. Despite the historical record, some Russian historians now claim that the Golden Horde never invaded Russia and that its leader, Batu Khan, was really the Russian hero Alexander Nevsky. Others favor the Eurasian theories of the unorthodox Russian historian Lev Gumilev (1912–92).

After the Mongols allied themselves with the Qing in 1691 they were forbidden to trade with Russia. The Qing were Manchu, but the Middle Kingdom was ruled by Han Chinese administrators and traders. The Mongols were impoverished, backward, and dying out, by the time of their declaration of independence in 1911. Russia took an interest in the Mongols, but in 1915 recognized China's claim to Outer Mongolia. The Bolsheviks' seizure of power in Russia in 1917, and their recognition of Mongolian independence, followed by their assertion of the rule of their Mongol counterparts in 1921, led to the launching of Moscow's first satellite state. The consequences of Soviet control included the rewriting of Mongolian history by the Soviet Communist Party (CPSU).

At the end of the Second World War the West accepted Stalin's offer to help end the Japanese Army's occupation of northern China in exchange for keeping Mongolia. For a while it was a Russian backwater, recognized

by the Republic of China, but after the victory of the
Communist Party of China (CPC) led by Mao Zedong
in 1949, the CPC and CPSU fell out, and the backwater
became the front line of ideological struggle and military
confrontation. In China's "cultural revolution" the
population of Inner Mongolia suffered greatly, the Mongol
leaders were exiled and traditional life disrupted. China's
resistance to Soviet "great power chauvinism" entailed
the reorganization of defenses, the redrawing of the
boundaries of Inner Mongolia and neighboring provinces,
and the displacement of the civil population away from
the international border.

The better to protect its slender lines of communication
across Siberia, the USSR strengthened the Mongolian
buffer's defenses, economy, and infrastructure. The
Kremlin fostered the USSR's image as the "elder brother"
(*akh*), always respected in Mongol society, and Mongolia
as the "younger brother" (*düü*) guarding the hearth, thus
defining their relationship as "fraternal" (*akh düü*). The
Mongols thought the Russians were contemptuous of
their religion and traditions, and drank too much.

When the Mongols asserted their freedom in 1990, they found that the polarization of their world, which had been East/West (Russia versus America), had reverted to North/South (Russia versus China), and there was resentment at Mongolia's almost seventy years of Russian occupation. There was dissatisfaction over alterations to their border, exploitation of Mongol natural resources, political persecution, the occupation of land for military use, and damage to the environment. Mongolia had lost over 30,000 people to Soviet-incited political purges, been deprived of its traditional *uigarjin* alphabet, and denied its own historical narrative, political freedom, freedom of conscience, and freedom of international dealings. Arguments about the benefits of long-term financial and economic aid and cultural development were undermined by Russia's demand for payment of a huge Mongolian aid debt in US dollars.

After the "cultural revolution" China gradually improved its relations with Mongolia. All the same, the Mongols still have reservations about China, fearing, as Deng Xiaoping is said to have envisaged, that after Hong Kong and Macao, one day Beijing might decide to recover "the lost territories" of Taiwan and Mongolia. Moreover, Mongolia's long historical and religious links with Tibet, in particular the Mongols' support for the Dalai Lama as their religious leader, contradict Beijing's rewriting of the history of Tibet.

The heritage of Manchu invasion and colonization and Chinese exploitation has left the Mongols with strong concerns about the risk of sinicization, whether by conquest or by commerce. Mongols dislike overseas Chinese (*khujaa*) and find it difficult to accept Mongol women marrying foreigners, especially Chinese men; real or supposed half-breeds (*erliiz*) are treated with particular contempt. China has always been considered a historical threat and challenge, while Russia was generally seen as friendly and supportive, despite the negative impact of communist rule, until the attitude of the "new Russians" of Putin's Russia changed this thinking.

The creation of the Shanghai Cooperation Organization by China and Russia in 2001 has become a challenge for Mongolia, which depends on both. It has observer status in the SCO, which it considers appropriate, but there have been calls by Russia and China for full membership. The symbol of the SCO, a dark blue half-globe depicting the member countries, surrounds Mongolia at the center in lighter blue! Aware of the fate of small nations at the hands of Putin's Russia and Xi's China, the Mongols continue building new partnerships in keeping with the "third neighbor" principal.

The "Third Neighbor"

In an effort to balance the influence of the two "eternal neighbors," Mongolia decided to pursue a "third neighbor" policy, its focus being on the United States, the European Union, and Japan, all three of which are politically influential and economically powerful. The Mongols had few political contacts with Europe in the medieval period—mostly Crusaders and papal representatives. For a while after Mongolia's 1921 revolution contacts were maintained with Germany and France, but then abandoned as the Soviet Union monopolized Mongolia's political and economic life. After the Second World War relations were established with Eastern Germany (the DDR), and other European satellites of the USSR, and economic ties through Comecon. Diplomatic relations were established with the German Federal Republic as well.

When Mongolia declared its independence from Qing China in 1911, its call for recognition by the United States and other countries was ignored, although there was a US mission in Kalgan, on the northern border of China. Had the United States acted positively at that time, the centenary of relations with Mongolia might have been celebrated in 2011! In fact diplomatic relations between the United States and Mongolia were delayed until 1987, largely because the US recognized the Republic of China (Taiwan), which had withdrawn recognition of Mongolia's independence in 1953. The UK was the first West European state to recognize Mongolia, in 1963.

US influence in organizations like the IMF ensured support for Mongolian economic development. Mongolia's soldiers received modern military training, and their blue helmets have participated in UN peacekeeping operations in various parts of the world, such as Afghanistan and Chad. Mongolia has also become involved in joint training exercises with the US Pacific Command, and signed agreements with various NATO departments, but in 2014 Mongolia rejected a reported US request for a base on Mongolian soil. US Presidents have visited Mongolia and vice versa, and US trade and academic institutions have taken root there. America has long been a magnet for young Mongols, and competition for entry into US universities is strong. The US ambassador is an influential figure.

Mongolia's old enemy Japan (creator of Manchukuo, initiator of the Battle of Khalkhyn Gol, occupying power in North China 1945), is now a new friend, partner, and important aid donor. The Japanese imagine themselves to be related to the Mongols, having a common ancestry and similar languages. Mongolia has found another important partner in South Korea, where as many as 80,000 Mongols have found domestic and other employment. Mongolia's links with North Korea are problematic, because of the idiosyncratic nature of the Pyongyang regime, but Mongolia still hopes to establish some kind of relationship that will promote its role as a go-between with Washington.

FROM BLOOD BROTHERS TO COMRADES

In Mongol and other nomadic societies patrilineal lineages were exogamous and kinship decided that only kin were allies. However, some flexibility was provided by blood brotherhood (*anda*). The associated ceremony or ritual (*andlakh yos*) involved the "blood brothers" (*and naiz*, sworn friends) drinking from a cup containing their mixed blood and pledging brotherly love and respect for one another. They would exchange gifts and might live for a while in the same *ger*. Blood brotherhood was an important way of forming alliances. Another was by becoming "marriage allies" (*quda*), that is, two men whose children had married each other. The tie was sometimes reciprocal, a father receiving a bride for his son then giving a bride for his ally's son. Genghis Khan was both an *anda* and a *quda*.

Friendship in present-day Mongolia distinguishes between acquaintances (*tanil*), and buddies or mates (*tünsh*), originally a business partner. The usual word is *naiz* or good friend, sometimes *naiz nökhör*; boyfriend is *eregtei naiz*, girlfriend *emegtei naiz*. The word *nökhör* in Genghis Khan's times meant "companion," used for the personal servants and bodyguards of the rulers. They were not only stewards, grooms, and quiver bearers, but also guard and troop commanders whose loyalty was paramount. In the modern era *nökhör* has come to mean "colleague," "comrade" in the political sense, and "husband."

Mongol friendships are formed among kin and, outside the family, at school or university. School reunions are important events, with reports and photographs in the media. Children make new friends at summer camps (*zuslan*).

MEETING THE MONGOLS

At the personal level the average Mongol is not much concerned about political issues, unless they affect business or personal life directly. Mongols appreciate it when foreigners try to communicate in Mongolian and want to learn their ways and customs, and don't mind when they make cultural or linguistic mistakes. They are interested in the wider world and new information from visitors, and are eager to learn about new techniques and technologies.

Foreigners can become friends with Mongols in the workplace or wherever else common interests are shared, such as at clubs and sports centers. They may make friends in focus groups on foreign affairs and language teaching, or in cooperation with religious and charity organizations.

Most first-time visitors to Mongolia, and foreigners receiving Mongol callers, are likely to be introduced by third parties who know the names and job titles on both sides and will deal with introductions. Shaking hands has become usual between men, and with some women. Mongols usually don't smile on first meeting or for photographs, and may seem initially uncommunicative, unless they speak English, which they may want to practice or show off.

Even if business is the main purpose of your meeting, to begin with the conversation should stick to generalities, perhaps sharing a common interest – football, horse racing, or golf. Do you share a hobby— fishing, perhaps, or stamp-collecting? Have you traveled abroad? Where do you go on vacation? Once you have established a common interest you might decide to eat together at a local restaurant. Where? What kind of food? Mongolian, Chinese, Korean?

The people you meet in rural areas will be quite different, having much less common ground with the casual visitor, although the advent of cell phones has changed things enormously. All the same, tradition is stronger here than in the cities, and people are closer to nature. Their main interest will be their family and livestock, and their food will be plain and traditional too. In the country, even casual meetings are likely to include an invitation to visit the family *ger*, but you are unlikely to be invited to stay without prior arrangement. In an emergency a neighbor not too far away may be able to put you up. You are the foreign visitor, you provide the entertainment! You will be given tea, koumiss, or vodka, chatted up, and when curiosity is satisfied, sent on your way. It will all be interesting, friendly and fun, but impermanent. Don't step on the threshold—it brings bad luck!

INVITATIONS HOME

As in other countries, home visits represent a step up from first acquaintance. In the city you will probably be taken in the owner's car, or driven there by a friend. Homes of course vary in size and quality, according to the owner's status and income.

When meeting the Mongolian family at home you may well be confused at first about who's who because many generations of the family may live under one roof. Begin by trying to get people's names right (see page 154). Most likely you will already know your host and hostess's names, but, if their children are old enough, get them to write down their names. Depending on the status of your hosts, you will decide how to address them (see page 153). Other people are bound to turn up to have a look at you, and will be introduced to you by name, so try to remember them, even if it takes some time to sort out who are relatives and who are friends. That elderly couple who live with the family are the youngsters' grandparents, but on which side? You could draw a family tree, and ask everybody to help with the relationships. You'll need a large sheet of paper—Mongolian family trees are drawn from the center outwards. Describe your own family, too. Draw your tree Western style, with each generation like a clothesline. Where do you live? Have you got a photo of your house or hometown, or a small map of your country, that you can show them?

If you are a new acquaintance your hosts may serve you minced mutton dumplings and vodka, and then sit back and watch you eat. That's Mongol hospitality. Care for the visitor comes first. When you know them better they'll probably eat with you. They will probably extemporize a toast in your honor, wishing you good health and a successful visit. You should respond in kind. Your response will be understood or translated for you, but you could surprise your hosts (and yourself) if you add in Mongolian, *"Erüül mendiin tölöö!"* ("Your health!")

In a *ger*, food is usually served at a low table, with stools to sit on. There will be various unsalted dried cheeses, creams, and pastries to nibble, all hard. While

cooked food is being prepared, *süütei tsai* (milky tea) is poured out and cigarettes and snuff passed around. The custom is to receive the snuff bottle in the right hand, admire its shape and decoration and, unless you take snuff, to sniff at it without opening it. The conversation will focus on the visitors, and there'll be enquiries about travel and weather conditions. The visitors should in turn ask after the health and wellbeing of the herder and his family and livestock.

DATING

Relationships with foreigners still tend to be frowned upon, although they are undoubtedly more frequent than they used to be. Mongolian families, once they get used to the idea, will probably welcome a foreign friend as readily as a Mongol one. Opportunities for privacy in Mongolia, however, are often quite limited.

The *Travellers' Language Guide for English-Speaking Visitors*, published in Mongolia (2006), is unusual in devoting a couple of pages to dating and flirting, from "Shall we go out together this evening?" through "You have a lovely smile!" and "I like you a lot!" all the way to "I'd like to sleep with you!" and "Only with a condom." (See also page 137.)

THE MONGOLS AT HOME

HOUSING

Until 1990 all buildings in Mongolia were built and owned by state enterprises or cooperatives. Apartments and urban houses were allocated to their occupants by local government bodies that charged nominal rents including the cost of electricity, water, and heating, which were unmetered. All citizens were required to register their residential address in their personal ID, which for many years was called an "internal passport."

During the 1950s and '60s collectivization of agriculture was completed, and the land, buildings, and equipment were owned by livestock cooperatives (*negdel*) whose members were paid mainly in kind but to some extent in cash; they were allowed to own a limited number of personal livestock. Crop-growing farmers were organized into state farms that were run like industrial enterprises and paid wages.

In the early 1990s, as the democratic revolution developed, rights of ownership were asserted and state-owned buildings privatized, beginning with housing. Most cooperatives and state farms disintegrated, and families or individuals registered as the owners of their dwellings free of charge. Later a market in housing developed, enabling people to buy and sell as they wished. Today property ownership is registered by the State Directorate of Registration and can be transferred and inherited. As water and power supplies were privatized, and apartment blocks had no electricity or water meters, the cost per building had to be divided equally among the owners by agreement. This applied also to repairs and maintenance, which many people could not afford, so that buildings completed in the 1950s and '60s to poor standards decayed badly, losing the plaster from the exterior walls and developing leaky roofs and peeling paint. Some residents formed voluntary associations to fund essential repairs.

When free distribution of land was introduced in 2003, the size of plots was regulated. Plots in urban areas were small, and those in rural areas larger, on the basis that people in the country subsisted on their land, while town dwellers did not. Most plot owners hoped to build their own homes. There is now a regulated free market in land and housing, and high-interest-rate mortgages are available. Properties range from large urban one-family houses (*khaus*) and Russian-style *dachas* (*zuslan*), to apartments (*bair*) in gated housing estates (*khoroolol*), or multi-occupancy buildings. The

urban poor live in small one-family houses, roughly
built wooden shacks, and *gers* in fenced compounds
(*geriin khoroolol*), often lacking utilities. The *gers* are
not regarded as real estate, and can be bought, sold,
or inherited free from inheritance tax.

According to the population and housing census in
2010, of the 713,780 households in Mongolia nearly
half were living in *gers* and just over half in permanent
buildings. Most households lived in privately owned
properties, but almost 210,000 lacked a water supply
or sewage system. Families living in *gers* numbered
around 157,000 in urban areas, while the number
living in rural areas was a little larger. Only 139,000
or so had mains electricity, 156,000 had a dried-dung-
or wood-burning stove for heating and cooking, and
128,000 a pit latrine. Ulan Bator had 633 water-supply
stations and 253 public bath houses. Of the 302,000 or
so households then in Ulan Bator over 100,000 lived in
apartments, 90,000 in single-family housing, and over
87,000 in *gers*. These statistics show that construction
of modern housing cannot keep pace with migration
into cities and the natural growth of the urban
population.

THE HOUSEHOLD

The 2010 census indicated that the size of the average Mongolian household was 3.6 persons (Ulan Bator 3.7), the largest households (Kazakh) being in Bayan-Ölgii province (average 4.4 persons). Women headed 24 percent of urban households, there having been a steady increase in the percentage of those divorced and separated and a decline in the percentage widowed. The proportion of divorced women is greater than that of divorced men, opportunities for women to remarry being poorer, according to an official report. The average age at first marriage in 2010 was 26.2 years for males and 24.2 years for females.

Between 2000 and 2010 the annual average population growth was 1.5 percent. In 2013 the number of households in Mongolia with four or more children under eighteen years old was 37,400, some 14,000 more than the year before.

DAILY LIFE

The lives of families living in Ulan Bator follow much the same pattern as the lives of British or American families. The working day in government offices begins at 8:30 a.m., in colleges at 7:40 a.m., and general education schools and kindergartens at 8:00 a.m. The staggering of hours is linked with traffic congestion.

Young children are used to walking to school or taking the bus on their own. Working parents take the bus, or drive in the family car, which needs a heated garage in winter. A family of this kind will be out all day, and eat their main meal in the evening. There may be a bakery just round the corner for light provisions, but for visitors a trip to a supermarket will show what goods are available. The cuts of meat may be different, but much else will be surprisingly familiar, including foreign brands. The womenfolk do most of the meal preparation and household chores; the men will drive when they go shopping.

In the capital you may notice many pawn shops (*lombard*). Most families have a few treasures or keepsakes, which they may have to pawn if they run short of cash meeting the demands of weddings, family reunions, or even longer-term commitments like children's or relatives' travel. Pawn shops are supervised by the city administration. The owners of goods being sold have to be given ten days' notice.

In rural areas everything is different. Life turns around the cycles of nature, not the clock. There is great freedom of movement, but wide empty spaces can be both safe and dangerous, and if anything goes wrong— you are thrown from your horse, or fall through the ice into a river—help or rescue may be far away. Children growing up in this environment are independent and used to being on their own, or in charge of younger siblings, and grow up with responsibilities for the care of young animals. Meal times depend on the work of the day, but the main meal is usually in the evening. Milky tea (*süütei tsai*) and pastry and cheese snacks are the usual daytime standby.

In summer the country people mostly eat "white" food—cream, curds, cheese—made from the milk of various animals, especially cows and sheep, but also goats, yaks, and camels. The cheese is dried on the *ger* roof in the sun, and becomes as hard as a rock. A sheep may be killed for a feast, but meat is mostly eaten in winter, when outdoor storage is easy and the diet requires more fat. In town beef and mutton legs brought by country relatives are hung out on apartment balconies. Don't be surprised if you see someone getting on a bus with a sheep's carcass!

A fine thing about country life is the night sky, with the Milky Way amazingly bright in the velvety darkness. You should have a flashlight with you, so shine it on the ground, and be amazed again, at how busy insect life can be after the heat of the day.

GROWING UP IN MONGOLIA

Resident grandparents make life easier for working parents by looking after their young (pre-school) children. They encourage proper behavior and the observation of Mongol traditions, and indulge them within these limits. Adolescent social life is no longer strictly controlled, beyond the involvement of youngsters in approved family social activity such as picnics and other outings. Teenagers and young adults are generally free to do as they please, within the family and clan standards they have been taught, and in most cases have some money to spend, ranging from pocket money to wages. However, young people do not have enough money to be independent, that is, to buy or rent accommodation or a car, and they usually continue to live at home with

their parents, even after marriage and the birth of their own children, whichever comes first.

The country's mass communist youth movement, the Revolutionary Youth League, run by the MPRP, was for a few aspiring politicians a stepping-stone toward membership of the ruling MPRP Politburo. The RYL broke up soon after the events of 1990, and the birth of political parties led to the foundation of their own political youth, student, and women's associations. The Scout movement was formed in Mongolia in the 1990s and has its followers. It is not particularly visible or influential, but the media praise Mongolia's Scouts as part of a worldwide brotherhood, and report their participation in international jamborees.

EDUCATION

September 1 is an important day, when schools reopen after the summer holiday for the first term of the academic year. Children and parents arrive at school with bunches of flowers for the teachers. Classes are mixed. Boys and girls wear standard dark blue uniforms and light blue shirts. Some schools are oversubscribed and have two half-day sessions, morning and afternoon. Because herders are often nomadic, children in country districts may board at their school during the week, returning to their families on weekends.

Pre-school education (kindergarten) is not available everywhere. Primary and secondary education is state-funded and universal, generally for eleven years from seven to eighteen, but parents have to buy workbooks and paper. Textbooks no longer have to be paid for, but school uniforms do, and parents complain about their cost and quality. There are now private schools like the British School and International School in Ulan Bator, but their fees are high.

Students studying in universities and colleges or receiving vocational training pay annual fees. Admission to higher education is thought by parents to be administered corruptly, so that despite open entrance examinations many places are said to be awarded in return for "informal extra payments." There is tremendous competition for entry into the best universities, colleges, and technical schools, some of which are privately run, and for scholarship places in foreign universities, especially where the teaching is in English. Some of these run joint colleges in Ulan Bator. (See also page 56).

HEALTH CARE

As in some other sectors, health services tend to be concentrated in the capital city, where most ordinary conditions can be treated to a high professional level at sixteen central and specialist hospitals. Elsewhere the situation is not good, although slowly improving. Foreign governments offer grants for clinic and hospital construction and equipment, sometimes in remote parts of the country, but provision of trained personnel is not part of the package. As a result medical facilities in rural areas may be modern but not in full use, or rudimentary, housed in decaying buildings. Industrial health has greatly improved, thanks to the provision of modern buildings and equipment with trained staff by international mining corporations.

Health services are provided by the state. Access for citizens is free, paid from national taxation and costing

6 to 7 percent of government expenditure in 2011–13, but patients are billed for many things..

People are encouraged to enroll in government and private health insurance schemes, paying in a percentage of their monthly income, any employer contributing half. Health insurance covers hospital stays, outpatient treatment, diagnosis, tests, and so on up to a fixed amount a year. Once the entitlement is exceeded the patient has to pay the difference. Medicines prescribed for outpatients have to be paid for, but common medications may be available at a discount. Citizens are entitled to receive emergency care, pre- and postnatal care, and treatment of some injuries whether insured or not. Corruption is said to be rife in the medical services and without a bribe doctors may withhold treatment of seriously ill patients. Treatment of limited access, such as dialysis, may also be available only on payment of a bribe.

In March 2015 there were 9,018 cases of HIV in Mongolia, a 14.5 percent rise year on year, and 185 of AIDS. Concern about the transmission of the HIV virus through the use of contaminated needles has resulted in much public interest in the crackdown on opium/morphine smuggling.

CONSCRIPTION

During the late socialist period, the length of service in the Mongolian People's Army varied according to the unit of recruitment and the educational standard of the recruit, but generally was three years. The weapons, technical equipment, and training were all Soviet. Only men were conscripted. After 1990 many things changed, including the country's political outlook and

Mongolia's foreign policy. Gradually the country opened up to military cooperation with countries other than Russia. The MiG fighters were broken up and scrapped, and the army reduced to about 10,000. Mongolian soldiers were trained for UN peacekeeping operations, and detachments were dispatched to Afghanistan and several countries in Africa. Regular field training was held with units of the US, Russian, Chinese, and other armies. New weapons and equipment were supplied by Russia, including T-72 tanks, but no military aircraft. The Mongolian Armed Forces established a general headquarters under a lieutenant-general; the president of Mongolia became commander-in-chief. New uniforms were designed, equipment was modernized, ceremonial guards and bands formed, and a sense of pride instilled in the conscripts. Military attachés were appointed to serve in some of the world's capitals, and the most promising young commanders are now sent to military colleges in the US and UK, not just Russia.

The new foreign policy led to the relaxation of conscription. In 2013 it was reduced to twelve months, although only about 30 percent of those called up are found fit for service. The call-up of all men aged eighteen to twenty-seven not studying or in a protected occupation is held twice a year, and is managed by the Ulan Bator district and *aimag* (provincial) military authorities. Women can serve, but are not conscripted. The government is improving the terms of service of regular volunteers to boost numbers and form professional cadres. The president has launched a program whereby students may complete two periods of military training in university vacations instead of being called up. A limited number of men opt to buy exemption from military service for about US $2,500.

chapter six

TIME OUT

To understand how Mongols spend their leisure, we have to consider once again the differences between the life of urban residents and that of people living in the countryside. City people have a clear picture of the difference between work and leisure, which is defined by their daily employment. With the exception of shift-workers who do night work, most urban residents enjoy public holidays and weekends free from work.

In rural areas life revolves around the care of livestock, and their twenty-four-hour need for protection, feeding, and watering. Country people tend to spend any free time watching evening television, and are likely to enjoy work-free periods only on traditional holidays, such as Tsagaan Sar and Naadam, and then only if the necessary cover for their temporary absence can be arranged with relatives or friends.

City people have more leisure time than their country cousins, but most of it tends to be spent at home, with the family, or going for outings as a family group, including small children, for picnics or barbecues in the nearby countryside. They tend to be quiet and reserved in public, as boisterous behavior is considered improper, especially that of noisy drunks. Eating out has become routine for the growing number of middle-class professionals, who tend to frequent restaurants serving Korean and other foreign food.

EATING OUT

Ulan Bator is well supplied with restaurants and hotels that offer a wide range of homegrown and imported foods and serve international cuisine, traditional Mongolian food, such as the delicious stews of meat and vegetables known as hot pots, and Mongolian barbecues. Most restaurants advertise Asian and European food. Pizza and other Italian dishes are particularly popular. It is even possible to find vegetarian, vegan, and organic restaurants.

There are several good Chinese restaurants, with Chinese staff and menus, the food prepared mostly northern style, as well as Indian and Korean restaurants. The *Mongolia Yellow Pages* also lists Russian, Japanese, Ukrainian, Czech, Turkish, and Thai restaurants, and one Uzbek. If you should ever be invited to a reception with a buffet, aim to collect your food early, or it will all be gone! It is not that Mongols are greedy; they enjoy events involving contact with foreigners and opportunities to sample what they consider to be "real" foreign food, and they will be hungry if it has taken them time to reach the venue.

Some restaurants display a short menu outside to attract customers. On entering you can choose where you want to sit, unless the restaurant is crowded, and a waiter or waitress will bring you the full menu. It may be quite lavish and in several languages, illustrated with color photos, from which you order dishes by their number. Smoking is not permitted in public places. Some restaurants, especially Chinese restaurants, have music, but it is not usually intrusive. Bars and fast-food outlets tend to be more noisy and crowded.

If no English is spoken, the now almost universal sign language of writing the bill, or waving a credit card, will draw the necessary attention. To call a waiter say "*Zöögch öö!*" ("Waiter!") In an emergency, "Help!" is "*Tuslaach!*" The Mongolian for "Yes!" is "*Tiim!*" and for "No!" is "*Ügui!*" or "*Bish!*" ("Not this, but that"). A general-purpose word in Mongolian that you will hear is "*Za!*" or "*Zaa!*" meaning "Well! Right! Sure! OK!"

Food is served at a good many bars. Local draught beers (Khan Brau and others) are available, along with bottled and canned beers from a variety of sources (Tsingtao, Kirin, Heineken). There is a big range of vodkas, but Scotch is popular among the Mongolian elite, and Bourbon may also be available. Gin and tonic can be obtained at most hotels, although the brand of tonic may be unfamiliar, and the barman unsure how to mix it. Over a hundred businesses in Mongolia are permitted to manufacture alcoholic drinks, and millions of liters are imported annually.

TIPPING

Some restaurants add a percentage service charge to the bill, but tipping is not traditional, and not expected in most cafés and bars. On the other hand, foreigners have been visiting Ulan Bator in some numbers for almost twenty-five years, so hotel clerks and restaurant waiters have begun to expect a small consideration. If you are particularly happy with the service you could leave a tip of up to 10 percent.

TRADITIONAL MONGOLIAN FOOD

In the summer country people mostly eat dairy produce, which is plentiful at this time of the year. Herders keep sheep, goats, and a few cows and horses, and make various kinds of cream, butter, and cheese from their milk. Potatoes, carrots, and cabbages are grown in many parts of the country, but the vegetable content of meals depends on what greens and root crops are available locally, along with wild onions, leeks, garlic, and herbs.

The national dish is boiled meat. This is usually mutton, up to half a sheep's carcass, boiled with its internal and external organs for several hours in a large bowl on the *ger* stove. The meat is eaten off the bone with a sharp knife. It is fatty and bland, but Mongols say that they can identify the locality where the animal was raised by its particular flavor. Beef is less common, owing to storage problems for the quantity of meat from one animal, but in some *gers* you will see strips of beef air-drying among the rafters. Pork is available in shops and restaurants, but not in the countryside, as pigs are not herded but raised on pig farms. Chicken, like pork, is available in town markets, but herdsmen do not keep poultry. Horse meat is rarely eaten.

Soups with a meat or vegetable base may contain flour

dumplings (*bansh*). Mutton dumplings, steamed (*buuz*) or fried (*khuushuu*), are juicy and tasty. The large deep-fried pastry *boov*, with crisscross patterns and roughly the shape of an inflatable rubber boat, are hard to chew. There may also be local berries, and fruit drinks like *chatsargana* (sea buckthorn juice). Mongols used to have excellent teeth and gums—strong enough to take the cap off a bottle of beer—but the young now eat too much sugar.

If you are traveling with hunters or anglers you can hope to benefit from their skills. There may be deer in the plains, boar in the forest, and duck in the lakes. Marmot (a fat rodent with a short bushy tail, which emits a high-pitched alarm whistle before disappearing into its burrow) has become rare, having been overhunted for its fur. Marmot with the bones removed, stuffed with hot stones, water added, and the carcass cooked in the campfire, is known as *boodog*. Alternatively, *khorkhog* can be made with layers of chopped lamb or kid and hot stones sealed in a cooking pot. Fish used to be avoided for religious reasons, but there are some fine catches to be had in Mongolia's northern rivers, especially the *tul* (Russian *taimen,* or Siberian salmon), four feet (120 cm) or more long. These are usually baked or barbecued.

DRINKS

Whenever you stop for refreshment in rural areas you are sure to be offered milky tea (*süütei tsai*) served in wooden

bowls. The tea is scraped from compressed bricks of Chinese tealeaves and boiled together with milk, butter, and salt and other ingredients, which may include fried flour. The tea content is rather small.

Mare's milk, or koumiss (*airag*), fermented in large

skin bags in the *ger*, is a nourishing food and refreshing but mildly alcoholic drink. Try it, but go easy, as it disagrees with some people. Vodka will most likely be offered, in small bowls or glasses, and toasts exchanged by hosts and guests. It comes in two varieties: clear, factory-bottled grain vodka (*tsagaan arkhi*), and cloudy, home-distilled milk vodka (*shimiin arkhi*), which some travelers find disagreeable because of its smell. At tourist *ger* camps a bar service is usually available, with bottled or canned beer. Everybody drinks bottled water. Check the seal on the screw top.

NIGHTLIFE

Gambling is banned. Mongolia's first casino, a joint venture called Mon-Macau, in the basement of the Genghis Khan Hotel, was about a month from opening when the Great Khural (national assembly) changed its mind about legalized gambling and banned it in January 1999. The minister of justice said that the country was "not ready" for a casino; the Great Khural disapproved of the "seedy side" of casinos—crime, prostitution, money laundering, and violence. Several of its members were arrested on suspicion of accepting bribes from Mon-Macau; the charges were proven and prison sentences of three to five years passed in October 1999. A police raid on a hotel near Ulan Bator railway station in 2014 led to the arrest of a company director, a department head at the Ministry of Mining, and a former MP, who were playing poker.

At the time of writing a casino bill was again in the legislation pipeline. For use by foreigners only, two casinos would be built in free-trade zones, possibly on the border with China, or at Ulan Bator's new airport at

Khöshigiin Khöndii. The cost was estimated at 35 billion *tögrög* (MNT) each, about US $18 billion, which is low by international standards, excluding hotel accommodation.

Meanwhile, there are plenty of nightclubs and disco/karaoke bars in Ulan Bator, to suit most tastes. The government has decreed early closing times for them, but fast-food outlets operate from 7:00 a.m. to 3:00 a.m.

CULTURAL LIFE
Music

The most popular Mongolian instrument is the horse-head fiddle (*morin khuur*), the player seated with the fiddle in his lap. The long neck curves at the tip into a carving of a horse's head, and the two strings are made from horsetail. The horse-head fiddle comes in a range of sizes up to the equivalent of a double bass, and features in folk music orchestras. Many families have one at home, as

a symbol of harmony. The *yataga* is a long, zither-like instrument whose strings are plucked, one end resting in the player's lap. The *shanz* is a three-stringed, long-necked lute, the *yoochin* a hammer dulcimer. Monastery musical instruments range from the conch-shell trumpet (*tsagaan büree*) to the long horn (*ükher büree*), a straight Alpenhorn. The music of these traditional instruments is evocative of Mongolian nature, embracing storms and breezes, rolling plains and high mountains, songbirds, melancholy, and love—an attractive combination that makes CD recordings popular souvenirs. Song, dance, and folk orchestra performances put on during the summer tourist season should not be missed.

Mongolian folk songs and dances are staged in Ulan Bator's State Academic Theater of Opera and Ballet by the State National Song and Dance Academic Ensemble, or the Tümen Ekh National Song and Dance Ensemble in the Children's Park. The Academic Ensemble staged its revival of the ballet *Legend of the Great Queens of Mongolia* in January 2015, the "saga of nine beautiful and wise queens"— about legendary figures and historical personalities such as the widowed Queen Mandukhai, who at the age of thirty married Batmönkh Khan, aged seven, to save the nation.

Mongolian folk dances include the bowl dance, in which the dancers balance small bowls of water on their heads, knees, or hands without spilling a drop. The *biyelgee* is a western Mongolian static dance suited to performance in a *ger*, the dancer half-sitting or cross-legged, presenting a pantomime of everyday life—milking, cooking, hunting, and so on, performed to the music of the *morin khuur* or *khulsan khuur* (bamboo jew's harp).

The Mongolian Philharmonic, and sometimes visiting foreign orchestras, perform European operas and classical concerts. These were introduced to Mongolia by the Soviets during the socialist period, but in effect opened up for the Mongols knowledge of European arts and culture. They remain popular among the intellectuals of the older generations, who do their best to educate their younger offspring in the world heritage. Performances tend to be announced at irregular and infrequent intervals, as the opera house is not open every day. Pop concerts are staged in summer in Genghis Khan Square.

Song
The 1921 revolution led to the destruction and loss of much of the Mongols' traditional cultural life. Modern songs, sometimes in traditional style, are composed and sung by folk choirs and professionals whose popular followers may sing or hum them.

Both traditional and modern songs in traditional style are short (*bogino duu*), light, and melodious, or long (*urtyn duu*), "as long and as wide as the steppe, reminding you of eternity and the vastness of nature," according to one performer. Long songs are now usually accompanied on the *morin khuur* or *limbe* (flute), but traditionally were unaccompanied.

Throat singing, or overtone singing (*khöömii*), is a technique from the Altai Mountains and Tuva in which the singer sings two pitches at the same time, one in the harmonic or overtone scale. The singer produces flute-like notes against a background drone in a series of harmonics. This requires the physical strength of a wrestler and lengthy training. It has been described as the representation of the entrancing sounds of a (perhaps mythical) flowing river, involving the spirits of the locality. Disapproved of by the lamas, *khöömii* was considered "music of the people" during the communist period. Some particularly skilled performers are said to be able to produce classical melodies by Tchaikovsky and Bizet.

The Mongols have a tradition of satirical songs about relations between men and women, often bawdy, called *kharganyn duu*, songs of the *khargana*, a desert shrub (where couples might hide). Some songs satirize relations between lamas. Dialog love songs are very personal, about people's shortcomings and improper relationships.

Theater

Mongolia's first modern theater was the Green Dome, which stood in what is now Genghis Khan Square in Ulan Bator. It became notorious in the late 1930s as the venue for the trial of "counter-revolutionaries"— Buddhist high lamas, the "class enemy" of Choibalsan's regime, but in fact innocent "victims of political repression." Traditional Mongolian theater dates back to the Buddhist plays of the poet and dramatist Ravjaa (1803–56), who was ordained as a Gobi incarnation and founded several monasteries. In 1831 he completed the morality play *The Moon Cuckoo*, based on an eighteenth-century Tibetan story, which became very popular, but was banned after the 1921 revolution. Buyannemekh (1902–37), who joined the MPP in 1921, wrote revolutionary plays in Chinese opera style, and a historical play about the boyhood of Temüüjin (the future Genghis Khan). Natsagdorj (1906–37) wrote plays and poems about the new regime's struggle against the "feudalists," as well as the libretto for an opera known in English as *Three Sad Hills*, which remains popular. The National Opera and Ballet Theater stages European operas in Mongolian.

Since 1990 there has been revival of temple dancing,

called *tsam*, which until 1937 was performed at monasteries by lamas dressed as fierce deities (*dogshid*). The genre was created by a thirteenth-century Tibetan lama and popularized in Mongolia in the seventeenth century as an annual religious performance lasting many hours. The dancers wear distinctive clothing and individual masks of papier-mâché. The performance ends with the exorcism of evil spirits.

Ulan Bator's State Academic Theater of Drama and the Mongolian Puppet Theater are housed in the large red building at the corner of Seoul Street. The mixed international repertoire includes Shakespeare and Chekhov, but usually in Mongolian.

Museums

Mongols are fond of their history and heritage, and interested in viewing associated exhibitions, whether of dinosaur fossils or antique religious paraphernalia. Buddhists spin the prayer wheels, light candles, and make offerings in temples to which the state has given the status of museum.

Choijin Lama Temple Museum

In the middle of town, the Temple Museum has begun to disappear among the new tower blocks. The residence of the Bogd Khan's brother, Luvsankhaidav, the State Oracle, this temple (1904–08) is famous for its collections of Buddhist paintings, *tangas*, sculptures, and papier-mâché *tsam* dance masks. The entrance is screened by a barrier gate (*yanpai*) to keep out evil spirits. The entrance hall is guarded by the massive figures of the Four Guardians (maharajas). The roof beams are decorated with portrayals of flaying, dismemberment, and other pleasures of the lords of the seven Buddhist hells—some of them cold.

Dinosaur Museum

The building near Genghis Khan Square temporarily housing a collection of dinosaur fossils, including several complete skeletons, used to be the Lenin Club, belonging to the former ruling MPRP. The top exhibit, a Tarbosaurus called T-Bataar, from the Gobi, was put on sale illegally in the US for $1 million, but was identified and claimed as Mongolian property.

A permanent museum is planned, and the Lenin Club may be refurbished as a Museum of Buddhism.

Zanabazar Fine Arts Museum

Named after the first Mongolian Öndör Gegeen (1635–1723), who was a gifted sculptor and artist, the museum contains four Buddha statues and other priceless examples of his skill. The museum stands on Builders'

Square (Barilgachdyn talbai) to the west of Genghis Khan Square. Zanabazar invented an alphabet for writing Mongol and Tibetan called the *soyombo* script, the first symbol of which was an abstract design representing the Mongol nation. The other exhibits include a mandala made of silver and gold thread and pearls, and the famous painting *One Day of Mongolia* by the nineteenth-century artist Sharav.

Museum of Political Persecution Victims

This large wooden house in German style, almost lost among the new high-rises of Olympic Street (Olimpiin gudamj) in central Ulan Bator, was where Prime Minister Genden lived before his arrest on false charges of spying for Japan and execution in Moscow in 1937. His house holds documents and photos of the dreadful years of political oppression under which some 30,000 people—statesmen, politicians, soldiers, and ordinary citizens, but many lamas—were arrested and executed by the communist regime. The children of victims of political oppression, granted compensation by the authorities, remember the victims at annual commemorations in September. There is a monument to the victims of repression near Genghis Khan Square.

The Military Museum, International Intellectual Museum (puzzle toys, logic games), Railroad History Museum (equipment of the Ulan Bator Railway), Ulan Bator City Museum (in a Russian house built in 1904) are all in central Ulan Bator. There is a Theater Museum too. Most museums apply price discrimination, that is, charge foreigners more than citizens for entrance tickets. The Museum of Natural History is closed for repairs at the time of writing.

Cinemas

There are several modern wide-screen and 3D cinemas in Ulan Bator that sometimes show American and British films, including the Tengis in Independence Square (*Tusgaar togtnolyn talbai*). Check Web sites: www.tengis.mn; Soyombo kino teatr www.soyombo. mn; Örgöö kino teatr www.urgoo.mn. Otherwise there are very few cinemas elsewhere in the country.

Circus

Ulan Bator's distinctive round circus building with its orange roof is not far from the former state department store (Ikh Delgüür). The circus ring and interior seating are rather neglected, perhaps because they are used infrequently—mostly by visiting foreign troupes. Mongolian circus acts were once popular, and famous for their contortionists. The circus is closed during the summer months, when the artistes are working abroad, and the building's circular passageways are used for clothing sales and charity events.

OUTDOOR ACTIVITIES

Although not natural team players, Mongolian competitors do well at individual sports like wrestling, judo, and taekwondo. Mongolia is proud of its Olympic sportsmen, who won three golds in the Beijing Olympics. There are fitness and sports clubs in the capital. Football (soccer) is popular, but largely non-participatory; fans know about British and European teams and leagues, and follow them in the popular media.

The Mongols are proud of their nomadic tradition, even though true nomadism, as once practiced, is now limited to seasonal movements of livestock. Mongolian horses are more the size of ponies, and are shod only if they are to be ridden on hard surfaces. There is a track for horse racing and trotting, but stabling in the capital is difficult. Pony trekking is popular with tourists.

Swimming is for summer, but there are few public pools, and youngsters mostly splash around in the local Tuul River, when it is full and clean enough. In winter there is skating, and areas of Genghis Khan Square are used as ice rinks. There are ski slopes with ski lifts and other facilities at the Sky Resort on Bogd Khan Uul.

As elsewhere, the political and business elite join the golf club in Ulan Bator for social contact and the nineteenth hole as much as for exercise and the club sauna. The greens need water, however, which is unpopular with the environmentally conscious.

Naadam—The National Sports Festival

Although the riders are children, horse racing is one of the three "manly sports" of Naadam, the national sports festival in July. The races take place across the open countryside near Ulan Bator, the distances run varying according to the age of the horses (colts, two-year-olds,

and so on). The horses, which are not given names, are distinguished only by their age, color, and markings, and the winners are the trainers. Some towns and district centers have their own Naadam at other times of the year. In the Gobi there are camel races and camel polo.

Wrestling and archery, the other two "manly sports," are best watched in July at the national stadium in Ulan Bator, although there is indoor wrestling at the Wrestlers' Palace in winter. The wrestlers wear red and blue briefs and long-sleeved jackets. The winner in each bout waves his arms at shoulder height simulating a *garuda* bird, the loser passing underneath. Various national anniversaries are marked with regional wrestling, usually with 256 or 128 wrestlers competing.

Sumo wrestlers have a strong following, particularly the Mongol wrestlers awarded Japanese titles, who are the country's top sporting personalities. "Yokozuna Hakuho" Davaajargal, named the sixty-ninth grand champion in Tokyo in February 2015, is a Merited Sportsman of Mongolia and Hero of Labor. The world championships will be held in Mongolia in 2016.

Compound wooden bows are used in traditional archery with blunt arrows, and the targets are stacks of leather cups placed on the ground at various distances; men and women compete separately. At Ulan Bator stadium you may see a display of mounted archery, the bowmen shooting at their targets from horseback. The craftsmen employed at Mongolia's only bow and arrow factory, at Dulaankhan in Selenge Province, use traditional materials and methods.

At Naadam you may also see competitions of "ankle-bone shooting" (*shagai*), which is registered with UNESCO as Mongolian intangible heritage. Also called "knucklebone shooting," it involves two players or two teams of players, who flick "bullets" from a launcher on their knee at rows of targets on a board.

SHOPPING FOR PLEASURE

At major Ulan Bator shopping centers like Central Tower Mall, Naran Plaza, and the Ikh Delgüür you will find all the famous international brands, such as Louis Vuitton, Hugo Boss, Swatch, and Chanel. Big shops accept international credit cards. A wide range of natural furs is available —hats, coats, and stoles—and sweaters, scarves, and gloves of Mongolian cashmere are good value.

The Ikh Delgüür is recommended for *deel*, embroidered jackets, traditional hats and boots; bows and arrows, wooden toys and puzzles; carpets and mats with Mongolian designs of animals, symbols, and Genghis Khan portraits; craft goods such as silver bowls, musical instruments, and wood carvings; Mongolian music and travel film CDs and DVDs, oil and water color portraits and landscapes; samples of calligraphy (old script); dolls in national dress, flags, and other souvenirs.

Souvenirs and "antiques" are also found at several shops in Tourists Road (Juulchdyn Zam), west of Genghis Khan Square. The export of antiquities, including fossils, is forbidden without an approved certificate of origin.

The old street markets, where sellers of every conceivable kind of secondhand tool, length of pipe, faucet, car part, and all sorts of domestic knickknacks, used to sit cross-legged on the ground with their goods displayed on a piece of felt, gradually disappeared as "modernization" replaced them with heated buildings and permanent stalls. Naran Tuul, once called the "black market," is one such, now specializing in traditional Mongol clothing, hats, boots, saddles and riding tack, *ger* parts, and souvenirs. There are some coin and "antique" dealers, too. It's sometimes very crowded, and thieves abound.

ATTRACTIONS IN ULAN BATOR
Genghis Khan Square (Chingisiin Talbai)

Ulan Bator's central square is dominated by a seated statue of Genghis Khan, set in the new multi-column south front of the State Palace, which houses the parliament, government, presidency, and the new national museum. At the center of the square stands a statue of 1921 revolutionary hero Sükhbaatar on horseback, facing the rising sun, his arm raised, greeting the dawn of communism. The square used to be called "platform square" (for public speaking) until it was named Sükhbaatar Square in the 1940s. The Mayor of Ulan Bator ordered the name changed to Genghis Khan Square in 2013.

The buildings around the square include the Opera and Ballet Theater and the Stock Exchange (a former cinema), as well as the Palace of Science, with neo-classical colonnades, and modern steel, glass, and concrete structures including Ulan Bator City Council and Blue Sky Tower.

From the 1950s to the 1980s the square was used for military parades and workers' demonstrations, as

in other communist capitals, but nowadays parades are rare and demonstrations voluntary. The square is busy year-round with sightseers, photographers, children's entertainments, and artists painting portraits and selling watercolors. The capital's new-year tree is set up there. The square is also the focus for pop concerts and viewing firework displays at other times of the year.

East of the square, on the north side of Peace Avenue (Enkhtaivny örgön chölöö), are the "Independence Palace," the HQ of the MPP, and Ulaanbaatar Hotel. A monument to Mongolia's national poet Natsagdorj (1906-37), which in 2013 replaced a statue of Lenin, stands in the gardens opposite the hotel.

Bogd Khan's Winter Palace

This complex (built 1889–1906) is situated a mile or so south of Genghis Khan Square, just off the road to Ulan Bator International Airport. It comprises structures of two distinct architectural styles: an inner series of ten interlinked Chinese-style temples and pavilions of one and two stories, containing Buddhist paintings and sculptures, with a ceremonial Chinese gateway (*pailuur*) at the eastern end; and a two-story dwelling in Russian style, with ornate carved window frames, built from blueprints provided by Tsar Alexander III. It houses the furniture, vehicles, and other possessions of the eighth Javzandamba Khutagt or Bogd Khan, the religious leader and King of Autonomous Mongolia from 1911 to 1924, and his queen, Dondogdulam. The island at the junction with the road to the airport is being developed to portray a caravan of lifesize pack camels in a desert-like environment; it used to be the site of a Second World War Russian tank, which has been moved to Zaisan.

Gandan Monastery

Northwest of the town center, the Gandan Tegchinlen
temple, in the inner compound, contains a self-portrait of
Zanabazar, statues of later incarnations of Javzandamba
(see pages 48–9), and Buddhist literature written in gold
on black paper. The neighboring temple has a statue of
Vajradhara, the primordial Buddha, true source of all that
exists including the other Buddhas, made by Zanabazar
in 1683. The nearby Dindinpovran (1838) was built as a

palace for the thirteenth Dalai
Lama when he fled the British
invasion of Tibet in 1902,
and is used by the current
Dalai Lama on his visits to
Mongolia. The tall building
(1911–13) on the north side of
the outer compound houses
a statue of Megzed Janraiseg
(Chenresi or Avalokitesvara,
bodhisattva of compassion),
86 feet (26.5 meters) high and
including great quantities of

copper, silver, gold, and precious stones. Completed
in 1996, it replaces the original, dismantled when the
monastery was being used as a Soviet barracks in
the 1930s and '40s, and reportedly sent to the USSR
for scrap, although it may have been put on display
in Russia.

Zaisan Tolgoi Lookout

This hilltop on the northern slopes of Bogd Uul is
dominated by a monument to Mongolian–Soviet
friendship, built in 1967, with a circular mosaic of
heroic figures, soldiers, farmers, workers, teachers, and,
a late addition, cosmonauts. It is floodlit at night. A bus
ride from town, and to the top, if you want to avoid
the steps, it provides a panoramic view of Ulan Bator:
the Tuul River and Moscow-Beijing railway line in the
foreground, the tall modern buildings around Genghis
Khan Square occupying the middle ground, and against
the mountain background miles and miles of small
houses and *gers*, with the Mongolian TV antennas and
power station chimneys poking up. Turn around, and
you may see deer grazing on the mountain slopes.
Local sights include a new Buddha park with a 58-foot
(18-meter) statue of Sakyamuni, the historical Buddha
who attained enlightenment and founded the Buddhist
faith. The country's top politicians have residences in
Bogd Uul's wooded valleys.

ATTRACTIONS OUTSIDE ULAN BATOR

Tsonjiin Boldog Genghis Khan Monument

This 130-foot (40-meter) statue of shiny metal depicts
Genghis Khan in armor on horseback and stands atop
a rotunda with thirty-six columns, representing the

descendants of the "golden family" from Genghis to
Ligden Khan (see pages 17–23). An elevator inside a
leg of the horse gives access to a gallery and short flight
of steps up the neck leading to the horse's head, where
a small platform has fine views of the local countryside
and *ger* camps. The rotunda contains a café, shops,
and the world's biggest Mongolian boot (*gutal*).

The monument is some thirty miles (50 km)
by road from Ulan Bator in the direction of Terelj
and Erdene district, at the spot where Genghis
Khan is reputed to have found a whip with a
golden handle.

Gorkhi-Terelj National Park
This is a vast national park, half of it forest, in Erdene
District, northeast of Ulan Bator. It has beautiful
scenery, interesting rock formations, and tourist
facilities. Access is by road from Terelj Valley, where
there are a hotel and *ger* camps. An eighteen-mile
(30 km) hike from Terelj (with a guide) is the ruin of
Günjiin Süm, a temple built in 1740 by her husband to
commemorate the death of the youngest daughter of
the Manchu Emperor Kangxi.

Great Maidar at Sergelen
Mongolia's tallest statue, a 175-foot (54-meter)
Maidar Buddha (Maidar, or Maitreya, the future
Buddha, a *bodhisattva* who, four thousand years after
Sakyamuni's passing, is expected to replace him on
Earth), is currently being assembled at Zürkh Uul
in Sergelen District, not far from Tsonjiin Boldog.
Construction will continue for a couple of years. When
complete the Maidar will stand in front of a 350-foot
(108-meter) *suvarga* (stupa) in a large park.

ATTRACTIONS ELSEWHERE
Amarbayasgalant Monastery
This, one of Mongolia's largest and most beautiful
monasteries, is situated in Selenge Province, west of
Darkhan. Founded in 1722 on the orders of Qing
Emperor Kangxi as a last resting place for Zanabazar,
it was completed in 1737. Zanabazar's remains
were taken there in 1778, and those of the fourth
Javzandamba joined them in 1815. The monastery was
badly damaged during the 1930s, but UNESCO has
helped to fund the restoration of many of the original
temples. Access is by a long road journey via Darkhan.

Karakorum and Erdene Zuu
These are the remains of the Mongol imperial capital
Karakorum (Kharkhorin), in the Orkhon Valley,
northern Övörkhangai. Genghis Khan gave instructions
for its foundation in 1220, but construction was begun
by Ögödei Khan. Access is by air, or a long road journey.
After the collapse of the Mongol Empire Karakorum
was destroyed by Ming troops in 1380. Important
archaeological finds by international expeditions at
Karakorum are on display in a fine modern museum.
Bricks, tiles, and stones from the extensive ruins
were used in the building of Erdene Zuu "yellow
hat" monastery, founded in 1585, with three temples
containing Buddha statues. Zanabazar transferred the
religious capital away from Erdene Zuu, which was
wrecked by the Oirat army in 1688. The monastery
was restored in the eighteenth and nineteenth centuries
and the boundary wall built with 108 stupas, but in
the 1930s the lamas were arrested or killed and the
monastery closed. The lamas have now returned, and
restoration of Erdene Zuu continues.

chapter seven

TRAVEL, HEALTH, & SAFETY

It was only in the 1950s that the trans-Mongolian Ulan Bator Railway was built, in Russian broad gauge, providing for transport of passengers between Moscow and Beijing (a week-long journey) via the Mongolian capital, although its main purpose was to transport freight. Now that the mining industry has become the key to Mongolia's development, planning and financing is in progress of new railway lines, of Chinese (standard) gauge and Russian gauge freight lines linking new mines with border crossing points.

The international trains, with either Russian or Chinese staff (and in Mongolia a Mongolian dining car), have three classes of travel: second or hard class (four persons per compartment), first or soft class (also four

persons), and deluxe class (two persons, shared shower cubicle on Chinese trains). Many second-class travelers bring their own food and drink. Fellow passengers in the dining cars tend to be curious and sociable with foreigners. The trains stop for up to fifteen minutes at intermediate stations, where berries, mushrooms, and preserves may be on sale by local people. Train travel is slow but interesting, and there's lots of natural scenery along the way.

Fifty years ago some urban roads were surfaced, but travel between the capital and outlying provincial centers by motor vehicle was cross-country, along established rutted routes. This was slow, consumed a lot of gas, which has to be imported, and damaged many vehicles. Since 1990 a network of hard roads has been under development to connect Ulan Bator with the provinces, financed by foreign grants and loans, and the situation is improving. Gas pumps and service stations have multiplied as car ownership has grown.

Good intercity bus services have been introduced; seat booking is necessary. Travel light, if possible, as buses tend to be full and laden with suitcases, backpacks, bales of wool, and so forth. If you want to visit outlying areas, however, you will need to rent a 4 x 4 and driver to get you over the mountains, through the dunes, and across the steppes, following the ruts.

TRAVEL
Passports and Visas
Under current arrangements, British passport holders can visit Mongolia for tourism or business without a visa for thirty days. US passport holders can visit Mongolia for business or tourism without a visa for up

to ninety days. If you want to stay for more than thirty days you must register with the Office of Immigration, Naturalization and Foreign Citizens. Your passport should be valid for six months from the date of entry. If you enter from Russia or China, you need to check their transit visa requirements. If you fly MIAT from Berlin to Ulan Bator you can pass across Russia as a transit passenger, as you can from London via Moscow with Aeroflot. Turkish airlines fly currently to Ulan Bator with a stop in Bishkek, Kirghizia. Korean Air flies from European airports to Ulan Bator via Seoul. If you visit Mongolia via Beijing, because of the timing of connecting flights you may have to stay overnight in China, for which a double-entry visa is required. In Mongolia carry your passport at all times, but keep a copy of it, with the Mongolian immigration stamp, in a safe place.

Air

Arrival at Chinggis Khaan International Airport, which is well organized and signposted, if rather crowded, is generally smooth. The airport is some twenty minutes' drive from the center of Ulan Bator. There are usually plenty of taxis, and a town bus service. A new airport for Ulan Bator, currently under construction somewhat farther away from the town center, will be of much greater capacity, and is expected to be ready in 2017.

The Mongolian airline MIAT flies to Europe (Berlin) twice weekly via Moscow, and to Tokyo and Seoul. The Russian carrier Aeroflot has several flights a week to and from Moscow. Korean Air flies to Seoul, and Air China to Beijing, Shanghai, and Hong Kong. Flights to provincial centers by Mongolian carriers (MIAT, Aero Mongolia, Easiness Airways, Khünnü) are the easiest way to travel to the more remote parts of the country, Uvs and Khovd

Provinces in the west, Khövsgöl Province to the north, and Choibalsan in the east. There may be only two or three return flights a week, but during the summer tourist season there are additional flights, and services to tourist centers like Karakorum, the ancient capital, and Dalanzadgad, in the Gobi, with desert camps nearby. Khünnü stopped its flights to Khövsgöl in March 2015, because of a fall in traffic following completion of the new main road from Ulan Bator to Mörön.

Train

The north–south single-track broad-gauge Ulan Bator Railway linking Moscow with Beijing runs through Ulan Bator. The Moscow–Ulan Bator journey takes five days and nights, the Beijing–Ulan Bator stretch two days. The towns of Darkhan and Erdenet have railway stations, but there may be only two or three passenger trains a day, depending on the season. Darkhan is on the main line, and Erdenet is the terminus of a branch line. Neither has an airport; they are business destinations rather than tourist centers. There are timetables at Ulan Bator station.

International trains tend to be booked up in summer. The infrequent local trains north to Erdenet and south to Choir and Sainshand are also used mostly by people on business. The lack of railway development and improvement of the roads encourages frequent travelers to take their merchandise by truck.

Road

Most journeys from Ulan Bator to outlying areas of Mongolia are by road, at least to begin with, and travel by comfortable bus is possible where hard highways connect the capital to the nearer provincial centers, like Tsetserleg, Khövsgöl, or Öndörkhaan (also called Chinges town). Standards of long-distance buses vary according to age and model, ranging from limousine coach comfort for the more expensive tickets to ex-public service vehicles with hard seats and luggage on the roof. Stops at district centers or gas stations may be hours apart, and toilet and washing facilities rough or nonexistent. Recorded music is probable, and recorded TV programs are possible (if you can see the screen), but there will be no vendors coming on board from a largely empty landscape. You might find a basic shop or two in a district center.

A new international bus station has opened at the Dragon travel center in Ulan Bator's Songinokhairkhan District, with services to forty-eight localities in sixteen provinces. There is a service from Ulan Bator to Ulan-Ude in the RF Buryat Republic, and a planned service to Ereen (Erlian) on the Chinese border.

For shorter journeys you can take a minibus, paying according to the distance. Minibuses carry a destination sign, but you may need help to ensure you get to the right one. If you plan to tour the countryside and visit *ger* camps, sign up with a company providing a suitable 4 x 4, guide, and driver. If you want to visit places in border areas, for example Genghis Khan's birthplace

at Gurvan Nuur, Dadal District, you may need a permit from the Border Protection Agency.

GETTING AROUND TOWN

Taxi

Ulan Bator taxis are painted in the firm's colors, display illuminated signs, and have meters. You can find a taxi at a taxi stand, or your hotel will call one. Currently taxis charge 1,500 *tögrög* (about 75 cents) per kilometer. Freelance taxi drivers (that is, private citizens) charge the same. Stand on the edge of the pavement on a busy road in a suitable place (not at junctions, traffic lights, bus stops, or pedestrian crossings), facing the oncoming traffic, put out your hand, and someone will stop to pick you up (at your own risk).

Having secured a cab, name your destination. There is a flat rate for frequently visited places. If it's complicated, ask an English-speaking Mongol at the hotel to write the instruction in Mongolian. Tipping is not expected, but freelance taxis are not metered. You will just have to consider whether the amount asked is reasonable. Mongols are generally honest.

Bus and Trolleybus

This is how most people travel to work and school. The Ulan Bator bus company is introducing pre-purchase travel smart cards to validate each journey, and single tickets may no longer be purchased from a conductor. Buses and minibuses run on fixed routes with destination signs. All buses are jam-packed in the rush hour.

Car

If your company does not provide a local vehicle you can hire one, with a driver. Self-drive is not yet an option for visitors. Insurance issues have yet to be resolved, driving conditions can be dangerous, and in rural areas, even with GPS, you would probably get lost. Main roads are generally good if properly maintained, but are subject to damage by rain storms and rock-slides, as well as blockage by grazing livestock and herds of wild deer, especially at night.

Rush-hour traffic in Ulan Bator is dense and slow-moving, even when private vehicle use is regulated by number plate—odds and evens banned alternately, free for all on Sundays. Driving too fast for the conditions, and drunk driving, kill a lot of people, especially in remote country locations. An ambulance helicopter was sent experimentally to a road crash for the first time in 2015. It is said that Mongolian drivers forget that they are not riding a horse, and imagine that the stopping distance of a car is the same.

On Foot

Many of Ulan Bator's attractions are in or near Genghis Khan Square; there are plenty of things to see, and plenty of places to shop, eat, or stop for a beer (see pages 101–2). Walking in town is quite safe, but the crowded sidewalks may be uneven, with covers removed from large drains. Where there are no footbridges, cross main roads at traffic lights or pedestrian crossings, and keep your eyes open for pickpockets at places where crowds form. In winter sidewalks are often slippery with ice. Some town roads flood easily because of poor or no drainage. In summer rain be careful when walking near large puddles—you cannot always be sure of the depth of water.

Addresses

The main road that runs east–west through Ulan Bator is called Peace Avenue (Enkhtaivny örgön chölöö), but the British and Russian embassies, which have been there for many years, insist on calling it by its earlier name, Peace Street (Enkhtaivny gudamj). Some street names were changed after the democratic revolution of 1990. Lenin Avenue was renamed Genghis Khan Avenue (Chingisiin örgön chölöö), Stalin Street became Seoul Street, and Marx Street was renamed Olympic Street. Gorky Avenue, named after the Soviet writer, became Ard Ayuush Avenue, after an early-twentieth-century Mongolian anti-Manchu resistance hero. Gagarin Street, commemorating the first Soviet cosmonaut (1961), and Brezhnev Street were renamed after Amarsanaa and Chingünjav, eighteenth-century anti-Manchu heroes. Leading up to Gandan monastery, Constitution Street celebrated the 1960 communist constitution, but has been renamed after Zanabazar, in honor of Mongolia's first Öndör Gegeen.

The main streets of central Ulan Bator are signposted in English as well as Mongolian, and street maps of inner Ulan Bator are available in English. The buildings are sometimes prominently named in Mongolian, but are not visibly numbered. Side streets are usually not signed, and may not even have a name. In the *ger* districts the roads and fenced compounds are numbered. Town addresses combine the named urban district (*düüreg*) and numbered sub-district (*khoroo*), plus the street name.

WHERE TO STAY

Ulan Bator has a full range of modern hotels of a high international standard with expensive restaurants; a number of modest family hotels with more limited facilities; and hostel-type accommodation for students and backpackers. Some of the mid-range hotels offer bed and breakfast only. There is a shortage of hotel accommodation in summer, and you should book early. Seek assistance if you want to book a room in a provincial hotel. Camping and hiking are options, but are best arranged with experienced guides, who will advise on the suitability of your planned excursion. Foreigners taking up employment in Ulan Bator will find long-term leases on offer in English-language advertisements.

In recent years the Mongolian capital has attracted several of the top-range international hotel chains. Ulan

Bator's oldest, more interesting, and most convenient
hotels are not the most expensive or luxurious, but are
comfortable and adequate, and not far from central
Genghis Khan Square.

Ulaanbaatar Hotel is the oldest (1960, refurbished)
but still the most conveniently central.

Chinggis Khaan Hotel is in Tokyo Street (Tokiogiin
gudamj), off Peace Avenue. Grander than the
Ulaanbaatar, it has the Sky shopping center at the back.

Bayan Gol Hotel, Chingisiin örgön chölöö, across
Peace Avenue, is friendly, and favored by tour groups.

Springs Hotel, Olimpiin gudamj, is small and
comfortable, with views of Genghis Khan Square.

Edelweiss Hotel, off Enkhtaivny örgön chölöö, is
small, in a quiet area, with a view of the Selbe River.

HEALTH
From the health point of view Mongolia is a safe place to
visit. No special inoculations are required, although your
tetanus shot should be up to date. If you plan to fish or
watch birds at the lakes, bring insect spray. Before you
leave home take out travel insurance that will guarantee

your repatriation. If you are taking special medication, bring a sufficient supply with you.

Medical services in Ulan Bator are good, and most hotels have a doctor or nurse on call. Local pharmacies have ready supplies of over-the-counter treatments for minor ailments, bandages, ointments, and so on. If you fall sick or are injured in Ulan Bator, your first port of call is probably the Korean Friendship Hospital in Peace Avenue (Enkhtaivny örgön chölöö), where English is spoken. Hospital and doctors' bills will have to be paid (by card or in cash) and reclaimed under your insurance when you get home. Keep all invoices, even if in Mongolian.

Dress appropriately to avoid heatstroke or frostbite. In winter warm outdoor clothing is needed, including thick-soled boots, double socks and gloves, and hats with earflaps. In Ulan Bator the tap water is drinkable, but bottled water is generally available. Simply as a result of your change of diet you may develop diarrhea, so you should bring suitable medication with you. It's also a good idea to avoid eating unwashed vegetables and fruit, and to wash your hands regularly. In restaurants that serve group meals, steer clear of salads set out on the tables before guests' arrival.

Natural Hazards

There are a few local diseases that will need treatment if you are unlucky enough to contract one. Approach dogs and other animals with caution in case they are rabid; if you are bitten by a sick animal wash the wound with alcohol and seek medical assistance. Outbreaks of bubonic plague occur in Mongolia from time to time, and you might find yourself in a quarantine area, but you will not be at risk unless you approach or touch a dead marmot carrying infected fleas. Tick-borne encephalitis is best avoided by using repellent, and in forest areas by rolling down your sleeves and tucking your pants into your socks or boots. Altitude sickness is possible even in Ulan Bator. If you are affected, allow yourself time to acclimatize. Avoid sunburn by using sunscreen and wearing a brimmed hat, and drink plenty of water. Drink alcohol modestly.

When driving cross-country wear your seat belt—dried-up river beds are not always visible and can be deep. When fording rivers check for depth and flow. Travel in daylight.

SAFETY AND SECURITY

Most crime in Mongolia is nonviolent, but petty crime is common in crowded places. Groups, including children and teenagers, sometimes harass pedestrians for money. Foreigners may be assaulted and robbed when walking at night in unlit streets, or using public transport or unlicensed taxis. International trains are used by smugglers. Seek advice from your embassy about the reliability of internal flights.

Possession and use of drugs is illegal. You will be recognized as a foreigner by your speech, dress, and behavior, so don't deliberately draw attention to yourself. It's polite to ask permission before taking photographs of individuals. Some temples discourage photography, especially if there are people at prayer; others charge foreigners flat rates for movie and still camera pictures.

Pickpockets range from the professional to the amazingly inept. In the street, at pedestrian crossings, and especially in markets, they will be after your wallet or passport. If they fumble so that you notice, shout in protest, but don't expect any help. A competent pickpocket will look much like everybody else and will seemingly just brush against you before disappearing.

The usual precautions apply. Don't carry cash or valuables you don't need, or leave them lying about in your hotel room; put them in the safe. It's safer to change money at a bank or exchange. Be particularly vigilant if you draw cash from a street ATM. So that you don't have to sort out a wad of notes in a public place you might find it useful, in the privacy of your hotel room, to look at Mongolian banknotes. Most of them have a portrait of Genghis Khan and look rather similar, though differ in color. There are no coins.

On the streets of Ulan Bator unemployed people make small charges for services like shoe-cleaning, measuring your weight, or making telephone calls, and even sell individual cigarettes. Homeless children, who live underground next to the city heating pipes, may beg for money, even in cafés, but you might consider giving them something to eat instead. This is just one facet of the social problems, arising from earlier population displacement and unemployment, that remain to be tackled.

Foreigners are sometimes cheated in bars or threatened for supposedly running up colossal bills, or enter into unwise personal negotiations with seemingly attractive young people. Some Mongolians drink excessively, become belligerent, and remember old prejudices against foreigners.

Don't forget that the full range of STDs has reached the heart of Asia. Mongols have been brought up with animals in the country and know all about sex, but on the whole they keep their opinions to themselves. They approve of loyalty, and gender equality in principle, but not of same-sex relationships, which were illegal until quite recently. On the Day of Tolerance 2014, the main speaker on LGBT issues was the US ambassador!

Other Risks
If you plan to skate or ski, climb mountains, trek over deserts, ride horses or camels, or fly on unscheduled flights, remember to check your insurance coverage first, and make arrangements with recommended tour companies.

chapter eight

BUSINESS BRIEFING

THE BUSINESS ENVIRONMENT

In recent years Mongolia's GDP growth has been falling, from 17.5 percent in 2011 to a projected 3 percent in 2015. Inflation is high. It was 9.3 percent in the first quarter of 2015. The US dollar–MNT rate has changed, from US $1=1,357 in 2012 to US $1=1,985 in 2015. In order to reduce deficits, the 2014 and 2015 budgets were both revised twice to cut government spending, including the dismissal of many civil servants from government agencies and state-owned enterprises, thirty-two of which were loss-making.

Foreign direct investment has declined because of international commodity market instability (the falling price of copper, coal, and oil), official disagreements with Oyuu Tolgoi and Tavan Tolgoi over taxation and partnerships, and uncertainty about the country's economic stability, growing indebtedness, and the prospect of a general election in 2016.

Despite the introduction of Millennium IT and assistance from the London Stock Exchange, the Mongolian stock exchange remains a small operation with low turnover. The 51.7 million shares traded in 2014 were worth 24.2 billion MNT, while trading in government securities amounted to 36.1 billion MNT: a total of 60.4 billion MNT (US $32 million). The number of registered businesses was 59,843.

The top companies by market value in 2014 were APU (alcohol and soft drinks), Tavan Tolgoi (coal), Berkh Uul (fluorspar), three other coal mines, Gobi (cashmere), and the State Department Store. Ex-director Demberel of the Chamber of Commerce and Industry, co-chairman of the Civil Will Green Party, in a letter to the Mongolian president, speaker and prime minister, described the Mongolian business environment as "miserable."

The country's leading industrialist, Chairman Byambasaikhan of the Mongolian Business Council, considers the negative international perception of government involvement in business to be a problem. Mongolia's mineral resources are valuable assets, but the government is poor at raising investment capital, poor at shareholder relations, and poor at project delivery and profit generation, he said. Some Mongolian businesses are run according to international practice, but the majority are not. There are concerns about government interference in business, the way the judicial system works, and the penalizing of business leaders. International business and lenders want to see the rule of law and the sanctity of the contract prevail in Mongolia. He added that it is important to have a fair judicial system that protects businesses.

Mongolia has substantial reserves of coal, gold, copper, and iron ore, as well as great potential in rare earths, uranium, and other minerals, but is hindered by its backward infrastructure. It depends on its two neighbors, Russia and China, for most of its trade, and has been trying for years to interest them in railway construction, which would vastly improve Mongolia's export potential via transit through China to Pacific seaports. However, progress has been hindered by the inability of successive Mongolian governments to settle domestic disagreements about railway gauges. Existing railways are of Russian broad gauge, and a broad gauge line is planned from Sainshand to link with the Eastern Railway via Choibalsan. The coal and copper mining companies want to build Chinese standard-gauge lines to China to export their products. In 2014 this question was resolved, in principle, but the railways still have to be financed and built.

Mongolia's "third neighbor" policy develops relations with political and economic competitors of Russia and China, including the United States, the EU, and Japan, and organizations like the OSCE and NATO. Foreign investors are concerned about the influence on Mongolia of its "eternal neighbors." The Mongolian government has long sought the construction of a Russian–Chinese gas pipeline through Mongolia, but it will be built from Siberia north of Lake Baikal to Manchuria, bypassing Mongolia. Despite discussion of plans for improved north–south road and rail links through Mongolia, there has also been talk of projected Russian–Chinese railway construction from western Siberia into Xinjiang, to link up with cities in central China, and from eastern Siberia across the Amur into Manchuria, also bypassing Mongolia.

DOING BUSINESS IN MONGOLIA

The Mongolian government has consistently said that it supports foreign direct investment (FDI), and the president and other senior officials have stated that foreign investment commitments will be kept and investor-friendly legislation passed. However, some investors consider that Mongolia's support for FDI remains an aspiration rather than a reality. Despite the reform of investment and other laws, they say that the resolution of disputes with Rio Tinto in accordance with the terms of the Investment and Shareholders Agreements and completing the development of the Oyuu Tolgoi gold and copper mine will explicitly demonstrate the Mongolian government's commitment to the transparent rule of law, sanctity of contracts, and free market principles.

The Invest Mongolia Agency (founded in 2013), or capital investment directorate—previously the foreign investment coordination and registration directorate of the former Ministry of Economic Development—is now under the direct supervision of the prime minister. Registration of companies and investors has been transferred to the Main Directorate of State Registration, under the supervision of the Ministry of Justice (so named in English to match EU practice, but in Mongolian it is the Ministry of Law). There have been several changes of ministry names and addresses since the government reshuffles of 2014. The Web site of the State Statistical Office provides monthly and annual economic information. The Montsame news agency publishes monthly and annual economic reports in English. Annual reference publications include the Oxford Business Group's *The Report: Mongolia*, and the Mongolia chapter in Routledge's *The Far East and Australasia*.

For the potential investor, there are a few reliable foreign sources of information about doing business in Mongolia. The UK Trade and Investment Web site deals under "Exporting to Mongolia," with issues such as benefits, challenges, growth potential, start-up and legal considerations, tax and customs matters, and business behavior, among other things. The generally perceived benefits of Mongolia include a fast-growing economic potential, freely convertible currency, and an increasing number of English speakers; and the strengths a well-educated population (97.4 percent adult literacy), a young population (over 81 percent under the age of forty) open to new ideas and products, and low utility costs.

The challenges range from Mongolia's landlocked position and dependency on world prices for its minerals, to shortage of professional skills, frequent amendment and inconsistent application of laws and regulations, and bureaucracy. One could add to the list the government reshuffle and restructuring at the end of 2014, which resulted in a large turnover of personnel in the civil service, including the diplomatic service. Mongolia's exports to the US in 2013 were worth only US $3.9m, but imports totaled US $512.7m.

The London-based Mongolian–British Chamber of Commerce has regular meetings with guest speakers on the subject of "Doing Business with Mongolia" (see page 165). Meetings draw top business executives experienced in working in Mongolia, as well as Mongol diplomats, officials, and traders. "Doing Business in Mongolia" at mongolia.usembassy.gov runs annual Mongolian Investment Climate Statements. Its nineteen chapters begin with openness to foreign investment, and via expropriation and compensation proceed to private ownership, transparency, investment, trade zones, etc., and statistics (see page 165). Talk to the commercial attachés at your nearest Mongolian embassy.

MANAGEMENT CULTURE

Mongolian private companies and state-owned organizations are hierarchical, and staff are disciplined. So-called "family" businesses are usually run by one boss, the senior partner, who may be male or female, and/or a politician. The recent introduction of a "glass" law on business transparency has meant that some information about personal earnings, and property ownership, is now in the public sphere, but the internal workings of management remain opaque.

Members of the Great Khural have considerable powers to influence the direction of growth of the national economy and individual sectors, and some of the older "Soviet" generation, MPs and businesspeople, are equivocal about the market economy and privatization. Mongolia has some fifty thousand private companies, mostly employing fewer than ten employees, and around eighty state-owned companies, almost half of which operate at a loss, and many of which employ thousands of workers. Despite the present coalition government's claimed intention to press ahead with privatization, since 2012 the number of state-owned companies and enterprises has actually risen slightly, perhaps because some influential people retain the old ideology, that state ownership is in the national interest. As a result, for example, it has proved impossible over the past twenty years to privatize the airline MIAT.

The Mongolian Trade Union Federation and its various subordinate union branches are much engaged these days in discussing labor protection issues, especially industrial safety, with employers' organizations. Wages and conditions are largely controlled by government legislation and demonstrations or strikes are infrequent. Trade union membership was obligatory during the socialist period, but rapidly declined after 1990. Ministries encourage business partnership agreements between trade unions and employers' associations.

CORRUPTION

Corrupt practices are still widespread and endemic, criminal and opportunistic. These are a legacy of the period of Soviet control, rather than of the traditional support system of clan membership and localism. According to the USAID mission to Mongolia, opportunities for corruption have increased at both the "petty" (administrative) and "grand" (elite) levels. Grand corruption is the more serious threat because it "solidifies linkages between economic and political power that could negatively affect or derail democracy and development."

Mongolia's Anti-Corruption Law of 2006 established an Anti-Corruption Agency, which in English calls itself the Independent Authority against Corruption (IAAC), as the principal agency responsible for investigating corruption cases. However, in 2013 implementation of the law was considered inconsistent, allowing corruption to continue at all levels of government. Contributing factors were conflicts of interest, lack of transparency, or of access to information, an inadequate civil service, and weak government control of key institutions. In 2013 Mongolia was 83rd out of 177 countries on the Transparency International Corruption Perceptions Index. Investigations are hindered by the immunity from prosecution of members of the Great Khural and dual membership of government ministers. A recent US embassy advertisement (in English) for the post of clerk/ interpreter at the embassy reminded applicants of "anti- nepotism issues" and other potential "conflicts of interest."

The IAAC has become very powerful, to the extent that former Prime Minister Altankhuyag occasionally complained about its investigations hindering the efforts of honest and hard-working politicians and businessmen. Annual tax returns of government and assembly officials are published, but the public knows little about the lives of leaders of the state sector and tycoons of the private business world. Some information is to be found in business directories, and business organizations hold annual competitions for the "top" directors. Companies are regulated by law and their activities are reported in the media.

PERSONAL RELATIONSHIPS

In business as in general, show people courtesy, praise what you like and appreciate, and make a point of thanking people who help you. If you need assistance, consider whom you should ask. Avoid burdening someone with tasks that would be unsuitable because of their lack of status or language skills, for example. Be careful not to seek favors that you might not want to reciprocate. Avoid critical observations of Mongolian customs or behavior that you dislike but cannot expect to influence. Heed advice in proportion to the knowledge and skills of the adviser. Give advice cautiously and appropriately, and don't tell people "this is how we do it." Avoid getting involved in discussions about local political or business personalities. Treat information given "in confidence" with caution. Don't drink too much!

Your first contact with Mongolian businesspeople may well be at a business conference at home or abroad, or as a member of a visiting delegation or interest group. When meeting for the first time, formality is important.

Men and women dress modestly. Men wear a suit, a long-sleeved shirt, and a tie, and women the equivalent in female business fashion. Give a firm handshake, but do not bow or act obsequiously; dignity is essential. Adopt a sincere and honest tone. Show respect for senior (elder) business partners. Eye contact is essential—avoiding it may suggest acute shyness, at worst discomfort or discontent. The older generation of businesspeople were educated in Eastern Europe, and their business style reflects Russian influence. The younger ones are increasingly educated in the West; they often speak English, usually understand Western business methods, and most are used to dealing with foreign partners. However, many Mongols consider Chinese partners untrustworthy.

Business Correspondence
It's unlikely that you will have any difficulties. Mongolian businessmen are familiar with correspondence in English, and there is no need to adopt any special approach if the company logo is at the letterhead. It is of course sensible to avoid the use of jargon or unusual abbreviations. You may need a specialist translator to deal with Mongolian technical correspondence, drawings, and the like.

MEETINGS
Most Mongolian businesspeople know about European business practices and habits and behave much as European businesspeople do: smiles, polite greetings, handshakes, and exchange of cards. Mongols don't smile as much as Europeans on first meeting, or when being photographed. Handshakes are seen by some as a foreign

custom and may not be offered. For forms of address, see page 153. Office meetings tend to be held at long tables, the two teams facing each other, with the senior representatives at the center of each row, and various aides at their sides. Out of politeness, top people in Mongolia tend to speak softly, so if there are no microphones, and you are sitting some distance from the action, you will have to listen carefully!

PRESENTATIONS

At business conferences and forums the organizers, in the rush to get through the day's listings, tend to forget the need to set aside time for questions and discussion. The delegates will be chatting with one another during the proceedings anyway. Some speakers will have created modern multimedia presentations, but others will stand at the lectern just quietly reading out their Mongolian texts.

Visitors wanting to do business in Mongolia should bring with them prepared electronic audio-visual presentations in English of what their company does and how it can work to a Mongolian partner's advantage. Mongolian business conference venues are set up to handle them. Presentations should follow a simple format, and end with a brief restatement of the most important issues, including contact details. Questions invited from the audience after presentations are sometimes lumped together thematically by the session chairman. If there is an appreciative

audience the presenter will be invited to further discussions.

Ministers and businessmen often speak good English, but may break into Mongolian if there is some problem with terminology. At big meetings and conferences there may be professional interpreters, with wireless earpieces supplied to delegates, and there may also be a microphone or two to pass to delegates for questions. Interpreters may have excellent colloquial English but little specialized knowledge about the subject matter, especially if it is technical.

NEGOTIATIONS

It is recommended not to begin negotiations with a detailed pitch or complicated presentation, which might give the impression that a quick decision is expected. It's better to have a general discussion between senior staff on the aims of the project and to leave the details to be worked out after agreement in principle has been reached. They will then take their findings back to the management. The final decision maker may not attend meetings until signing is agreed. Signing lots of papers at an early stage gives the wrong impression. If possible, seek advice from locals who may know the people you are dealing with, and suggest known areas of special interest to your would-be customer. Negotiations across

the table will be concentrated but not formal. This is an oral culture, often meeting without an official agenda or minutes, but with the negotiators' aides taking notes.

CONTRACTS

Contracts are important, usually drawn up as two documents: one in English and one in Mongolian. However, once signed they may still be challenged, ignored, or misused, and there will be accusations by competitors of "secret clauses" and "special deals." Sometimes there is confusion over the interpretation of contracts or regulations.

Resolving Disputes

Sometimes officials in charge of government projects leave for another job elsewhere and take the documents with them, causing problems for those needing to complete the project. Difficult discussions and disagreements should never involve direct accusation or contradiction of the Mongolian partner, especially not in front of others. Exchanges of that kind are best restricted to suitably private moments.

In the event of disagreement about implementation of a contract, if differences cannot be resolved at meetings between the parties, local arbitration managed by the Mongolian Chamber of Commerce may be the next course to follow. Big companies, with large investments at stake, turn to international arbitration.

Travel Bans

Mongolian public and private entities may use administratively imposed travel bans to press foreign investors to settle civil disputes. Immigration officials may impose a travel ban pending criminal investigations, resolution of civil disputes, or for immigration violations. Exit is not allowed until the dispute is resolved administratively or a court renders a decision.

THE SGS TRIAL

At the end of January 2015, US citizen Justin Kapla, and two Filipinos, Hilarion Cajucom and Cristobal David, were tried in Ulan Bator and sentenced to five years in jail on charges of evading US $6.8 billion in taxes. They were employed by SouthGobi Sands, a subsidiary of the Canadian SouthGobi Resources in which Rio Tinto is a stakeholder. Their offices were raided by the Mongolian authorities in May 2012, but the investigation dragged on for three years, during which the accused were barred from leaving Mongolia and their bank accounts frozen. The formal charges against them, brought in May 2014, were denied, and Kapla filed a complaint with the UN High Commission on Human Rights. Although the case was a civil action, the prosecution surprised the court by calling for sentences of imprisonment under criminal law.

The US ambassador Piper Campbell, who attended the SGS trial, said that because of inadequate interpretation, the defendants had been unable to understand the proceedings or to express themselves clearly. The Chairman of the American Chamber of Commerce in Ulan Bator, Jackson Cox, who also attended, commented that the trial outcome made it hard to talk about investment and stronger trade.

WOMEN IN BUSINESS

In Mongolia women are not treated differently from men, and the business world is no exception. There are plenty of Mongolian businesswomen, but rather few in high management positions in large corporations. Some have leaped to prominence in the new, free-market Mongolia. J. Oyuungerel, the founder of Petrovis, took over NIK, the main importer of refined petroleum, developed an oilfield, and set up an insurance company. She was nominated for several business awards between 1995 and '98 and proclaimed Top Woman 1999 by the Mongolian Chamber of Commerce and Industry.

Garamjav, the founder of Monpolimet, a gold-mining company, who was educated at Moscow State University, and majored in international minerals and contract law in Rome, was elected a Secretary of the MPP in July 2012. Mongolian businesswomen tend to move toward politics.

Saule, a Mongolian Kazakh, joined the MPP leadership in 2007 and was made deputy minister of food, agriculture, and light industry in 2008. She is now Secretary of the MPP's Chamber of Advisers.

BUSINESS GIFTS

Don't give anything big or expensive; it's the gesture that counts. Your company's branded goods, ties, and pens will be a hit. Wrapped gifts are usually not opened in the presence of the giver, and generally little fuss is made. It's best to accept gifts with quiet dignity. Follow the Mongolian custom of giving and receiving with the right hand. Take some English paperbacks for the interpreters, and notebooks and ballpoints for the children if visiting a colleague's family.

chapter **nine**

COMMUNICATING

LANGUAGES AND SCRIPTS
Mongol
Mongol is the official language of the country, and its
Khalkh dialect is spoken by 80 percent of the population.
Other dialects of Mongol are spoken in neighboring
countries. As we have seen, it is a Ural-Altaic language,
and resembles Turkish. With a Mongol teacher the
language is not difficult to learn, but it is time-consuming
and hard to speak well.

Over the centuries Mongol came under foreign
influences from Tibetan, Manchu, Chinese, Russian, and
now English, adding to the vocabulary words such as
the Tibetan *lam* (monk), Manchu *zangi* (commander),
Russian *mashin*, and English *biznes*. Russian was
once compulsory and is still understood by the older
generation. English is taught in Mongolian schools and
is the foreign language of choice.

Written in columns, top down, left to
right, the Mongol script, or *uigarjin*, was
developed in the thirteenth century from
the writing of captured Uighur scribes.
It remained in use down the centuries,
preserving archaic forms. In the 1930s,
Stalin instructed Soviet linguists to devise
Latin alphabets for the USSR's national
minority languages. The Latin script for Buryats and

Kalmyks was adopted by the Mongolian authorities. As it was about to be introduced in 1940 Stalin decided that modified Russian Cyrillic alphabets would be more patriotic. With two extra letters for front vowels, Cyrillic was widely introduced in Mongolia in 1945 and remains in general use. Books and documents in *uigarjin* were placed in closed archives, and *uigarjin* ceased to be taught in Mongolian schools. After the birth of democracy in 1990 use of *uigarjin* was encouraged, but Cyrillic was retained for everyday use. The vertical script is now mostly used for decoration in diplomatic credentials, citations and certificates, a few publications, and public signs. A controversial new Language Law adopted in 2015 may widen its use. Romanized Mongol Cyrillic, launched in 2003 and revised in 2012, has not become an established standard.

Kazakh

Mongolian Kazakhs speak a dialect of the same Altaic language as the Kazakhs of Kazakhstan, and until the development of a modified Cyrillic script for Kazakh they wrote in Arabic script. Kazakh is not an official language in Mongolia, and the Kazakhs use Mongol in communications with the authorities. The Tannu Uriankhai (Tuvans) also speak an Altaic language, and while Uriankhai was part of Outer Mongolia they used *uigarjin* for written communication. Tuvan was not written until a Latin script was introduced in 1930 and a modified Cyrillic script in 1940.

ADDRESSING MONGOLIANS

On formal occasions one refers to and addresses politicians or businessmen by their full name and title:

President Tsakhiagiin Elbegdorj, or Mongolian Great Khural Chairman Zandaakhüügiin Enkhbold. Otherwise they are usually addressed by title: Prime Minister, Minister, Chairman, Ambassador, and so on. "Mr." is *noyon*, before the name, and "Mrs." is *khatagtai*, after the name, but note that a married woman keeps her own name; she doesn't adopt her husband's. In the Mongolian phrase for "Ladies and gentlemen," the words are sometimes transposed—ladies don't always come first: "*Noyod khatagtai nar aa!*"

You will please your Mongolian contacts if you greet them in Mongolian, "*Sain baina uu*?" (pronounced "sign buy-n oo") meaning "Are you well?" The reply is "*Sain, ta sain baina uu*?" "Fine, are you fine?"

NAMES

Mongolian personal names are formed differently from European names. Mongols have three names, their clan name (*ovog*), patronymic, or father's name (*etsgiin ner*), and given name (*ner*), in that order. A person is known by his or her given name, which serves as a surname would in official documents, directories, and other lists. Thus Ganbold is also Mr. Ganbold, but his wife is not Mrs. Ganbold, as she has her own name. The patronymic is formed from the father's given name and a possessive suffix, such as Sükhiin Ganbold, his father's given name being Sükh. An initial for the patronymic helps to distinguish between people with the same given name: S. Ganbold.

Clan Names

Clan names (*ovog*) were banned as feudalistic by the communist government in 1925, and for over sixty-

five years the word *ovog* was used for the patronymic
instead. The banning of clan names and family trees led
to the gradual loss of clan memory and raised fears of
accidental inbreeding with close relatives. In a reversal
of this policy, the 1996 Law on Culture called for the
keeping of family trees in accordance with government
rules. The rules specify that "all citizens must use three
names: given name (*ner*), father's name (*etsgiin ner*), and
clan name (*ovog*)" in the "citizen's passport" (internal ID),
foreign travel passport, birth certificate, family register,
national census, and other forms of registration. From
the age of sixteen a person can change his or her given
name and *ovog* by reregistration. Lists of clan names are
published to help people who have no record of their
clan name. With some 1,300 to choose from, people can
select an appropriate *ovog* from the part of the country
where their family originated. Mongolia's cosmonaut
Gürragchaa chose Sansar (cosmos). The most popular
ovog turned out to be Borjigon, the clan name of
Genghis Khan.

Given Names

Mongolian given names (*ner*) are drawn from a variety
of sources—the names of planets, days of the week,
flowers, and desirable personal qualities and features.
Men's names like Bat (firm), Ganbold (steel), and Tömör
(iron), and women's names like Narantsetseg (sunflower),
Oyuun (understanding), and Delgermaa (rich) are
typical. So as not to attract the evil eye, superstitious
parents once used to name a child "fierce dog"
(Muunokhoi), or "not this one" (Enebish). Names with
the suffix —khüü (son) are common: Altankhüü (golden
son), Baatarkhüü (hero son). Children may be named
after their day of birth, Lkhagva (Wednesday) or Baasan

(Friday) from Tibetan, or their Sanskrit equivalents, Bud and Sugar (Mercury and Venus). Tibetan names usually have a religious connection: Dorj (*rdo-rje*, *vajra*, thunderbolt), Maidar (Maitreya, the Buddha to come), and Molom (*mon-lam*, blessing). There are Sanskrit-based names like Ochir or Vachir (as Dorj) and Erdene (jewel). Mongol Kazakhs have distinctive names, reflecting the Muslim world: Akhmed, Khusein, Soltaan, and names ending in -bai, -bek, and -khan: Seregbai, Khurmetbek, and Zardykhan.

In Mongolian alphabetical order, simple given names (Bat, Sükh) are listed first, followed by hyphenated compounds (Bat-Üül, Sükh-Erdene), and then unhyphenated compounds (Batbold, Sükhbaatar).

"Surnames"

The Western media reacted to the legislation on family trees and clan names by running stories about Mongolians "being given surnames." Unfortunately, when the State Registration Agency issued new internal identity cards and passports, it equated *ovog* not with the clan name but, as before, with "father's name" and with the English translation "surname." Moreover the "father's name" was printed without the suffix (as in Ganbold Sükh), meaning that personal documents contain two given names. Mongolian patronymics precede given names (for example, Sükhiin Ganbold), whereas English surnames follow given names. As a result, there can be confusion about which name is which, especially when name cards are printed in English with two given names. Some Mongolian publications in English render President Tsakhiagiin Elbegdorj's name as Elbegdorj Tsakhia, which they would never do in Mongolian. A feature by a Mongolian journalist about the former Ambassador to the US, Khasbazaryn Bekhbat, named him Ambassador Khasbazar all through!

HUMOR

Mongolian humor covers a range of possibilities. Under socialism the authorities tried, partly successfully, to institutionalize and politicize humor. In the early years of democracy nationalist themes became popular, while portraying Mongolia as a poor and isolated country. One popular range of cartoons portrays life in Mongolia today as a replay of a famous late nineteenth-century painting, "One Day of Mongolia," making fun of officials, pompous people, and drunks. Cartoonists have since turned their attention to corruption, overt wealth, and the plight of the poor. Cartoons of politicians are mostly limited to so-called "friendly sketches." Humor at the expense of Russia or China is rare. Irony is not a popular quality.

A Mongolian comedian has categorized the subjects of Mongolian jokes as follows: difficult mothers-in-law, secret lovers, muddles and mistakes, old women, recycled old jokes, Twitter and Facebook stories, and conversations between drunks and policemen. In newspaper cartoons animals talk to one another, often retaining their well-known fairy-tale characters. Mongolians like multilingual puns: *mori-sarlag* (horse-yak) is "cognac," from the Russian *kon'-yak*.

In the socialist period a fortnightly satirical magazine called *Tonshuul* (woodpecker), like the Soviet *Krokodil*, served the purpose of political propaganda, making fun of "backward" behavior in its own country, and criticizing Western countries and politicians. There was "unofficial" humor, too. The name of the Mongolian People's Republic (in Mongolian, Bügd Nairamdakh Mongol Ard Uls, acronym BNMAU) was rephrased by humorists as "Let's all go to my place and drink vodka!" ("*Bügderee niileeg manaid arkhi uuya*"). The Russian equivalent, MNR (Mongolskaya Narodnaya Respublika) was "*Mozhno ne rabotat!*" ("No need to work!")

Mongolian Jokes

On his way to school young Enebish finds a hedgehog and puts it in his satchel. He shows it to his teacher, and she calls the class together to look. "What animal is this?" Nobody knows. "Surely you must know," the teacher says, "there are lots of poems and songs about it." "Miss," says Enebish, "is it a Lenin?"

A forester catches a young angler: "Fishing is not allowed here, my lad!" Boy: "I wasn't fishing!" Forester: "So what fish is this?" Boy: "This is my pet fish. I'm giving it an outing. I put it in the water and as soon as I whistle it comes back, then we can go home." Forester: "OK, show me!" The boy puts the fish back in the water and they wait. Forester: "So, whistle then!" Boy: "Why?" Forester: "Your fish didn't come back!" Boy: "What fish?"

THE MEDIA
Broadcasting

Radio broadcasting in Mongolia was introduced under the communist government in 1933 to provide the population with ideological guidance as well as information. Mongolian Television, which began broadcasting in 1967, served the same purposes. After the birth of democracy in 1990 the media diversified under private business and party political leadership, but the role of state-owned Mongolian Radio and Television continued ambiguously. A law on public broadcasting adopted in 2005 converted MRT into Public Radio and Television but it remains government-funded. During the post-election riot emergency in Ulan Bator in 2008 all broadcasters except PRT were taken off the air.

Mongolia has 142 television stations and 72 radio stations. The principal broadcaster is the former state-owned National Public Radio and Television, which has several radio programs and two TV channels and the greatest reach across the country. People in the cities receive TV from cable companies, which have 278,000 subscribers (2013). In rural areas TV is received with satellite dishes linked to solar photo cells and batteries.

Quiz shows, interviews with pop stars, and films ensure that television is the main source of entertainment, with national and international newscasts, some summarized in English. TV stations transmit up to twenty hours a day, TV-9 for twenty-four hours a day. TV broadcasts may also be received from China, Russia, and Kazakhstan, and some European countries. TV is being digitalized, and analog transmissions will cease in 2016.

Local radio stations play a lot of pop music, but include traffic news and weather reports. A BBC World Service English relay operates in the Ulan Bator area.

The Press

Most people these days get their news and comment from TV, while the press provides political and business commentary for an educated urban audience. Daily newspaper print-runs and circulations are quite small, and the large number of different newspapers is disproportionate, reflecting a wide range of good and bad taste. Most people buy subscriptions to their publications from the post office, now that street newspaper sellers have become rare. Some bookshops have news stands.

As of mid-2014, Mongolia had 123 national and local newspapers, and 98 journals and magazines. Several "daily" newspapers, most of which print five or six editions a week, represent the party political core of the print media, expressing views of the main political parties, the DP, MPP, and MPRP.

The largest circulations are claimed by *Ödriin Sonin* (Daily News) with 9,000 per edition and *Önöödör* (Today) 6,300. They both have Internet sites (DNN and Mongolnews respectively). The oldest newspaper, *Ünen* (Truth), belongs to the MPP, which founded it in 1920. *Ardyn Erkh* (People's Power) is linked with the Web site www.news.mn, including English pages.

The much larger number of weekly, fortnightly and thrice-monthly newspapers have smaller circulations and constitute the popular (*shar*, or yellow) press, concentrating on crime, scandal, international soccer, wrestling, cooking, and the lives of local pop singers and Hollywood film stars. The provinces and provincial cities publish at least one weekly newspaper.

Journals available range from Mongolian-language editions of *National Geographic* to English-language publications like the *Economist*. There are two English-language weekly newspapers, the *Mongol Messenger*, published by Montsame news agency, and *UBPost*, published by Mongolnews; both are available on the Internet. Montsame also publishes weekly newspapers in Russian, Chinese, and Japanese, and in *uigarjin* script.

Freedom House classifies the Mongolian media as "partially free," mainly because of the lack of freedom of information legislation and the use of libel legislation by the powerful. Broadcasters and newspapers are owned and backed by business groups, some linked with politicians. The World Press Freedom Index for 2015 raised Mongolia's index by thirty-four places to 54th out of 180 countries, the biggest jump of the year.

SERVICES
Telephone

In 2014 Mongolia had 210,400 landlines, 175,500 of them in Ulan Bator. Landline numbers typically are of six digits, preceded by a two- or three-digit district code. The usual code for Ulan Bator is 11, but there are others, including 21 and 51; hotels and tour guides usually print a full country list. The country code for Mongolia is 976.

Over four million cell phones were registered in 2013, more than one per head of the population. It's no longer remarkable to see, in a desert area of southern Mongolia miles from the nearest telephone pole, a lone camel-rider chatting away on his phone. Coverage across the country is still uneven. The market leader, Mobicom, and Unitel use the GSM system; Skytel is no. 2, and with G-Mobile uses CDMA. NetCo operates the national network.

Mail

If staying in Mongolia, you may receive mail addressed to your hotel or business, or by arrangement *poste restante* at the central post office. Mongols have their own local post office mailboxes, which are in great demand. Problems with addresses and the demand for boxes explain the popularity of cell phones.

Postal addresses are based on the mailbox (*shuudangiin khairtsag*) number and the number of the local post office (say, Ulaanbaatar-13), where mail may be collected from rented mailboxes. The first steps have been taken to introduce five-figure zip codes. They begin with the number of the province or capital. Ulan Bator is 1. UB's Sükhbaatar *düüreg* is 14, and Baga Toiruu, the inner ring-road, for example, is 14021. Mailboxes are being installed in building entrances and housing areas, and in some places there are parcel collection boxes with electronic keys.

Internet

The number of regular Internet users in 2014 was estimated at 762,000, the vast majority of whom were urban dwellers (essentially UB, Erdenet, Darkhan, plus a few provincial centers). There are about 11,120 miles (17,900 km) of optical fiber cable, and 150 rural district centers (about half) are on the network. Residents of Ulan Bator have access to the Internet via cable service providers. Wireless service areas are being created in hotels. There are many Internet cafés.

CONCLUSION

Mongolia's development of its mining industry has encouraged foreign direct investment and broadened its ties worldwide. Hillary Clinton has described it as the "torch of democracy in Asia." It has been building economic and political cooperation with the US and EU, OSCE, and NATO, but it is an observer of the Shanghai Cooperation Organization, of which Russia and China are key members. Its foreign trade is dominated by China, in particular coal exports. Exports to Russia are small; the chief imports from Russia are machinery and oil. Once Mongolia's planned refinery is operational, its dependence on Russia may be reduced.

However, Mongolia depends on Russia and China for freedom of access, and may be less important to them than they are to it. Once an ally of Russia and buffer against China, now it is dependent on China. Having mended its relations with China, Russia has less need for Mongolia, and Russia and China could cooperate more closely in developing their Eurasian interests while bypassing it. In 2017 Mongolia is due to pay the first US $500 million tranche of its "Genghis" government bonds issued in 2012. All the more reason to settle its internal and external disagreements over the Tavan Tolgoi coalmine and Oyuu Tolgoi copper and gold mine and boost investment and economic growth.

The Mongols proudly compare their achievements with those of other countries, while at the same time promoting their country's culture in the field of intangible world heritage through UNESCO. Great store is set on world development indicators. As a result of years of Soviet influence, they still measure national success in terms of livestock herds, coal exports, trade balance, and GDP, as well as the ownership of cell phones and motor cars, indeed the growth of the population itself, which surpassed three million in 2015, and life expectancy. The Mongolian media proudly publish data showing the country five points ahead of, say, Sudan, in standard of living tables, or eight points behind Russia for crime and corruption.

Mongolia sees itself, perhaps unrealistically, as the heartland and future leader of a greater Mongolian world, embracing at least spiritually the Mongols of Chinese Inner Mongolia, Xinjiang, and Tibet, the Buryats and Kalmyks of Russia, and numerous smaller Mongol communities across the world. Paradoxically, it also wishes to be thought of as part of the European world. To some extent Sovietization has Europeanized the Mongols of Mongolia, making their transition into the global community that much easier. The Mongols want to remain free and independent, in so far as that is possible for a landlocked state, but their leaders, struggling to maintain sustainable economic progress, have had to remind them of the reality of their permanent neighbors, and of the need to respect them.

Mongolia is an emerging third-world society, seeking its own proper place in the world, and has many advantages over other competitors for foreign support, if only its leaders could agree on their efforts to take the country forward. The Mongol people are steady and resourceful, but also somewhat inexperienced in the face of the choices imposed on them by globalization. Make the effort to connect with them on a personal level, however, and you will find them warm, tough, pragmatic, adaptable, hospitable, and open to the world.

communicating

Further Reading

Atwood, Christopher P. *Encyclopedia of Mongolia and the Mongol Empire.*
New York: Facts on File Inc., 2004.

Batsukh, J. and O. Chinzorig. *Secrets of Mongolian Business Leaders.*
Ulan Bator: Top Secret Newspaper, 2007.

Bruun, Ole. *Precious Steppe: Mongolian Nomadic Pastoralists in Pursuit of the Market.* Lanham, MD: Lexington Books, 2006.

Danzan, Narantuya. *Religion in 20th Century Mongolia.* Saarbrücken: VDM Verlag Dr Müller AG, 2008.

Diener, Alexander C. *One Homeland or Two? The Nationalization and Transnationalization of Mongolia's Kazakhs.* Redwood City, CA: Stanford University Press and Woodrow Wilson Center Press, 2009.

Dierkes, Julian (ed.). *Change in Democratic Mongolia: Social Relations, Health, Mobile Pastoralism and Mining.* Leiden: Brill, 2012.

Kaplonski, Christopher. *Truth, History and Politics in Mongolia: Memory of Heroes.* Abingdon: Routledge, 2004.

Pegg, Carole. *Mongolian Music, Dance and Oral Narrative.* Seattle: University of Washington Press, 2001.

Rossabi, Morris. *Modern Mongolia: From Khans to Commissars to Capitalists.* Berkeley, CA: University of California Press, 2005.

Sanders, A. J. K. *Historical Dictionary of Mongolia.* Lanham, MD, and London: Scarecrow Press, third edition 2010.

Sanders, A. J. K., with J. Bat-Ireedüi. *Mongolian Phrasebook and Dictionary.* Victoria: Lonely Planet, third edition 2014.

Weatherford, Jack. *Genghis Khan and the Making of the Modern World.* New York: Crown Publishers, 2004.

Useful Web Sites

National Chamber of Commerce and Industry, Ulan Bator: chamber@
mongolchamber.mn   www.mongolchamber.mn
American Chamber of Commerce (AmCham) (official affiliate of the US
Chamber of Commerce): info@amcham.mn   www.amcham.mn
Mongolian–British Chamber of Commerce: www.mongolianbritishcc.org.uk
Contact john.grogan@mongolianbritishcc.org.uk
Tourist information offices are to be found at the Central Post Office, Ulan Bator
railway station, and Chinggis Khaan International Airport's Arrivals:
www.welcome2mongolia.com/touristinfo

culture smart! mongolia

Index

culture smart! mongolia

Acknowledgment

With grateful thanks for my wife Tina Tamman's support and forbearance.